LEVITICUS

Chapters 1—14

J. Vernon McGee

THOMAS NELSON PUBLISHERS

Nashville • Atlanta • London • Vancouver

Published in Nashville, Tennessee, by Thomas Nelson, Inc.

Scripture quotations are from the KING JAMES VERSION of the Bible.

Library of Congress Cataloging-in-Publication Data

McGee, J. Vernon (John Vernon), 1904–1988
   [Thru the Bible with J. Vernon McGee]
   Thru the Bible commentary series / J. Vernon McGee.
     p.   cm.
   Reprint. Originally published: Thru the Bible with J. Vernon
McGee. 1975.
   Includes bibliographical references.
   ISBN 0-7852-1006-7 (TR)
   ISBN 0-7852-1072-5 (NRM)
   1. Bible—Commentaries. I. Title.
BS491.2.M37 1991
220.7′7—dc20   90–41340
                                      CIP

PRINTED IN MEXICO

11 12 13 14 – 03 02

CONTENTS

LEVITICUS—CHAPTERS 1—14

Preface v

Introduction vii

Outline xiii

Chapter 1 15

Chapter 2 27

Chapter 3 37

Chapter 4 47

Chapter 5 61

Chapter 6 71

Chapter 7 81

Chapter 8 89

Chapter 9 103

Chapter 10 109

Chapter 11 119

Chapter 12 137

Chapter 13 145

Chapter 14 165

Bibliography 179

PREFACE

The radio broadcasts of the Thru the Bible Radio five-year program were transcribed, edited, and published first in single-volume paperbacks to accommodate the radio audience.

There has been a minimal amount of further editing for this publication. Therefore, these messages are not the word-for-word recording of the taped messages which went out over the air. The changes were necessary to accommodate a reading audience rather than a listening audience.

These are popular messages, prepared originally for a radio audience. They should not be considered a commentary on the entire Bible in any sense of that term. These messages are devoid of any attempt to present a theological or technical commentary on the Bible. Behind these messages is a great deal of research and study in order to interpret the Bible from a popular rather than from a scholarly (and too-often boring) viewpoint.

We have definitely and deliberately attempted "to put the cookies on the bottom shelf so that the kiddies could get them."

The fact that these messages have been translated into many languages for radio broadcasting and have been received with enthusiasm reveals the need for a simple teaching of the whole Bible for the masses of the world.

I am indebted to many people and to many sources for bringing this volume into existence. I should express my especial thanks to my secretary, Gertrude Cutler, who supervised the editorial work; to Dr. Elliott R. Cole, my associate, who handled all the detailed work with the publishers; and finally, to my wife Ruth for tenaciously encouraging me from the beginning to put my notes and messages into printed form.

Solomon wrote, ". . . of making many books there is no end; and much study is a weariness of the flesh" (Eccl. 12:12). On a sea of books that flood the marketplace, we launch this series of THRU THE BIBLE with the hope that it might draw many to the one Book, *The Bible*.

J. VERNON MCGEE

The Book of
LEVITICUS

INTRODUCTION

Many years ago, I read a statement by Dr. S. H. Kellogg saying that he considered the Book of Leviticus the most important book in the Bible. I felt that he must have had his tongue in cheek to make a statement like that. Then I heard a great preacher in Memphis, Tennessee, Dr. Albert C. Dudley, say that he considered the Book of Leviticus the greatest book in the Bible.

Several years ago I made an experiment on our radio program, and actually I didn't know what would happen as I began teaching this book. I wanted to study it and I wanted to see if it was such a great book, and I must confess that I had misgivings as to the value of Leviticus for a popular exposition on the Bible. However, I discovered that it is a thrilling book, and not only that, but I can now honestly say that I consider the Book of Leviticus one of the most important books of the Bible. If it were possible for me to get the message of this book into the hearts of all people who are trying to be religious, all cults and "isms" would end. A knowledge of the Book of Leviticus would accomplish that.

The Book of Leviticus was written by Moses. It is a part of the Pentateuch, the first five books of the Bible.

In the Book of Leviticus, the children of Israel were marking time at Mount Sinai. The book opens and closes at the same geographical spot, Mount Sinai, where God gave the Law. You will remember that Exodus concluded with the construction of the tabernacle according to God's instructions and then the filling of the tabernacle with the glory of the Lord. Leviticus continues by giving the order and rules of worship in the tabernacle. Leviticus is the great book on worship.

The book opens with the Hebrew word *Vayick-rah*, which means "and He called." God has now moved to the tabernacle and speaks from there; He no longer speaks from Mount Sinai. He calls the people to meet with Him at the tabernacle. He tells them how they are to come and how they are to walk before Him. The exact meaning of the church, the *ekklesia*, is the "called out ones." We are also those who have been called out. In that day, God spoke from the tabernacle and asked them to come to Him. Today, the Lord Jesus calls us to Himself. He says, "My sheep hear my voice" (John 10:27). So this book has a wonderful message for us today.

Leviticus is the book of worship. Sacrifice, ceremony, ritual, liturgy, instructions, washings, convocations, holy days, observances, conditions, and warnings crowd this book. All these physical exercises were given to teach spiritual truths. Paul wrote: "Now all these things happened unto them for ensamples: and they are written for our admonition, upon whom the ends of the world are come" (1 Cor. 10:11). In 1 Corinthians 10:6 he says, "Now these things were our examples . . .". "For whatsoever things were written aforetime were written for our learning, that we through patience and comfort of the scriptures might have hope" (Rom. 15:4).

Peter tells us that the Old Testament holds spiritual truths for us. "Of which salvation the prophets have inquired and searched diligently, who prophesied of the grace that should come unto you: Searching what, or what manner of time the Spirit of Christ which was in them did signify, when it testified beforehand the sufferings of Christ, and the glory that should follow. Unto whom it was revealed, that not unto themselves, but unto us they did minister the things, which are now reported unto you . . ." (1 Pet. 1:10–12). Hebrews 11:13 says, "These all died in faith, not having received the promises, but having seen them afar off, and were persuaded of them, and embraced them, and confessed that they were strangers and pilgrims on the earth."

Leviticus has some wonderful instruction for us today for it reveals Christ in a most remarkable manner. Tyndale, in his *Prologue into the*

Third Book of Moses, said, "Though sacrifices and ceremonies can be no ground or foundation to build upon—that is, though we can prove nought with them—yet when we have once found Christ and his mysteries, then we may borrow figures, that is to say, allegories, similitudes, and examples, to open Christ, and the secrets of God hid in Christ, even unto the quick: and can declare them more lively and sensibly with them than with all the words of the world."

Worship for us today is no longer by ritual or in a specific place. You remember that the people of Israel had been going through ceremonies and they had their rituals, but Jesus said to the woman at the well in Samaria, ". . . Woman, believe me, the hour cometh, when ye shall neither in this mountain, nor yet at Jerusalem, worship the Father. Ye worship ye know not what: we know what we worship: for salvation is of the Jews. But the hour cometh, and now is, when the true worshippers shall worship the Father in spirit and in truth: for the Father seeketh such to worship him. God is a Spirit: and they that worship him must worship him in spirit and in truth" (John 4:21–24).

The keynote to the book is holiness unto Jehovah. The message of the book is twofold:

1. Leviticus teaches that the way to God is by sacrifice. The word *atonement* occurs 45 times in this book. Atonement means to "cover up." The blood of bulls and goats did not actually take away sin. It covered over sin until Christ came to take away all sins. This is what Paul is referring to in Romans 3:25: "Whom God hath set forth to be a propitiation through faith in his blood, to declare his righteousness for the remission of sins that are past, through the forbearance of God."

The sins that are past are the sins back in the Old Testament. You see, God never accepted the blood of bulls and goats as the final payment for sin, but He required that blood be shed. It was an atonement to *cover over* the sins until Christ came. In other words, God saved "on credit" in the Old Testament. When Christ came, as the hymn accurately states it, "Jesus paid it all." This is true as far as the past is concerned, and as far as the present is concerned, and as far as the future is concerned.

One of the key verses in Leviticus, dealing with atonement, is found in Leviticus 17:11, "For the life of the flesh is in the blood: and I have given it to you upon the altar to make an atonement for your souls: for it is the blood that maketh an atonement for the soul." The way to God is by sacrifice and without the shedding of blood, there is no remission of sins.

2. Leviticus teaches that the walk with God is by sanctification. The word *holiness* occurs 87 times in this book. "And ye shall be holy unto me: for I the Lord am holy, and have severed you from other people, that ye should be mine" (Lev. 20:26).

God gave strict laws governing the diet, social life, and daily details involving every physical aspect of the lives of His people. These laws have a greater spiritual application to His people today. That is the reason I think we ought to study Leviticus. You see, access to God is secured for the sinner today through the shed blood of Christ. The writer to the Hebrews stated it this way: "Nor yet that he should offer himself often, as the high priest entereth into the holy place every year with blood of others; for then must he often have suffered since the foundation of the world: but now once in the end of the world [literally, end of the age] hath he appeared to put away sin by the sacrifice of himself" (Heb. 9:25–26).

Those who are redeemed by the blood of Christ must live a holy life if they are to enjoy and worship God. "Now the God of peace, that brought again from the dead our Lord Jesus, that great shepherd of the sheep, through the blood of the everlasting covenant, make you perfect in every good work to do his will, working in you that which is well-pleasing in his sight, through Jesus Christ; to whom be glory for ever and ever. Amen" (Heb. 13:20–21).

Leviticus is a remarkable book, as the contents are considered in the light of the New Testament. This book is about as dull as anything possibly could be to the average Christian and you won't find very many classes or individuals reading and studying the Book of Leviticus. Yet, it is a remarkable book.

1. The five offerings which open this book are clear, crystal-cut cameos of Christ. They depict His hypostatical person in depth and His death in detail (chapters 1—7).

2. The consecration of the priests reveals how shallow and inadequate is our thinking on Christian consecration (chapters 8—10).

3. The diet God provided for His people was sanitary and therapeutic, and contains much spiritual food for our souls (chapter 11).

4. Attention is given to motherhood and is a further example of God's thinking concerning womanhood (chapter 12).

5. The prominence given to leprosy and its treatment, in the heart of this book on worship, demands our attention. Why is there this extended section on leprosy? Those who have been given gracious insights into Scripture have found here a type of sin and its defiling effect on man in his relation to God. The cleansing of the leper finds its fulfillment in the death and resurrection of Christ as typified in a most unusual sacrifice of two birds (chapters 13—15). My friend, if you and I would escape the defilement of sin in this world, we need to know a great deal about the death and resurrection of Christ and the application of it to our lives.

6. The great Day of Atonement is a full-length portrait of the sacrifice of Christ (chapter 16).

7. The importance of the burnt altar in the tabernacle highlights the essential characteristic of the Cross of Christ (chapter 17).

8. The emphasis in this book of instructions concerning seemingly minute details in the daily lives of God's people reveals how God intends the human family to be involved with Him (chapters 18—22). God wants to get involved in your business, in your family life, in your social life. My friend, let us beware lest we shut Him out of our lives.

9. The list of feasts furnishes a prophetic program of God's agenda for all time (chapter 23).

10. The laws governing the land of Palestine furnish an interpretation of its checkered history and an insight into its future prominence. There are a lot of prophecies in this book. The nation Israel and the Promised Land are intertwined and interwoven from here to eternity (chapters 24—27).

There is a relationship in the first three books of the Bible:

In Genesis we see man ruined.

In Exodus we see man redeemed.

In Leviticus we see man worshiping God.

We can also make a comparison and contrast between Exodus and Leviticus. In the Book of Exodus we see the offer of pardon; Leviticus offers purity. In Exodus we have God's approach to man; in Leviticus it is man's approach to God. In Exodus Christ is the Savior; in Leviticus He is the Sanctifier. In Exodus man's guilt is prominent; in Leviticus man's defilement is prominent. In Exodus God speaks out of the mount; in Leviticus He speaks out of the tabernacle. In Exodus man is made nigh to God; in Leviticus man is kept nigh to God.

OUTLINE

I. **The Five Offerings and the Law of Them, Chapters 1—7**
   A. Sweet Savor Offerings (Person of Christ), Chapters 1—3
      1. Burnt Offering (Christ Our Substitute), Chapter 1
      2. Meal Offering (Loveliness of Christ), Chapter 2
      3. Peace Offering (Christ Our Peace), Chapter 3
   B. Non-Sweet Savor Offerings (Work of Christ on Cross), Chapters 4—5
      1. Sin Offering (Sin as a Nature), Chapter 4
      2. Trespass Offering (Sin as an Act), Chapter 5
   C. Law of the Offerings, Chapters 6—7

II. **The Priests—All Believers Are Priests, Chapters 8—10**
   A. Consecration of Priests, Chapter 8
   B. Ministry of Priests, Chapter 9
   C. Restrictions on Priests; Death of Nadab and Abihu, Chapter 10

III. **Holiness in Daily Life—God Concerned with His Children's Conduct, Chapters 11—22**
   A. Food of God's People, Chapter 11
   B. Children of God's Children, Chapter 12
   C. Cleansing of Leprosy, Chapters 13—14
   D. Cleansing of Running Issues, Chapter 15
   E. Great Day of Atonement, Chapter 16
   F. Place of Sacrifice; Value of the Blood, Chapter 17
   G. Application of Commandments to Life Situations, Chapters 18—20
      1. Immorality Condemned (Amplification of Seventh Commandment), Chapter 18
      2. Social Sins (Application of Commandments), Chapter 19
      3. Penalty for Breaking Commandments, Chapter 20
   H. Law for Personal Purity of the Priests, Chapters 21—22

IV. **The Holy Holidays, Chapter 23**

V. **Laws and Prophecies for the Promised Land, Chapters 24—26**
   - A. Lampstand, Showbread and Death Penalty for the Blasphemer, Chapter 24
   - B. Sabbatic Year, Year of Jubilee, and Law of Kinsman-Redeemer, Chapter 25
   - C. Conditions of Blessing in the Land (Prophetic History), Chapter 26

VI. **Dedication and Devotion—Concerning Vows, Chapter 27**

CHAPTER 1

THEME: The burnt offering; regulations, ritual, and reason for the burnt sacrifice; the law of the burnt sacrifice

This is the oldest offering known to man. It was the offering of Abel, Noah, and Abraham. All the offerings were made on the brazen altar but because the burnt offering was made there, the brazen altar is also called the burnt altar. It received its name from this sacrifice. This offering is recorded first of the five offerings because of its prominence and priority. This offering is a picture of Christ in depth as well as in death. A man cannot probe the full meaning of this offering because it sets before us what God sees in Christ. We can't see as much as He does. Here is a profound mystery that only the Holy Spirit can reveal.

The burnt offering shows the person of Christ. He is our substitute. Paul reveals this in Ephesians 5:2: "And walk in love, as Christ also hath loved us, and hath given himself for us an offering and a sacrifice to God for a sweet-smelling savour."

REGULATIONS FOR THE BURNT SACRIFICE

And the LORD called unto Moses, and spake unto him out of the tabernacle of the congregation, saying [Lev. 1:1].

God called unto Moses out of the tabernacle. No longer is He speaking from the top of Mount Sinai in thunder and lightning, as when He gave the commandments. Here He calls to Moses from the tabernacle in reconciliation.

"And the LORD called"—His call is for those who will hear His voice. That is important to see. God is calling to men today to be reconciled to Him. The church is a called-out body, and they are the elect because they are called. "For the Jews require a sign, and the Greeks seek after wisdom: but we preach Christ crucified, unto the Jews a stumblingblock, and unto the Greeks foolishness; but unto them which are called, both Jews and Greeks, Christ the power of God, and the wisdom of God" (1 Cor. 1:22–24).

"Called" doesn't mean those who only hear; it means those who have heard and responded. I would like to ask you this question: Have you heard Him and have you responded to Him?

Speak unto the children of Israel, and say unto them, If any man of you bring an offering unto ᴜᴇ LORD, ye shall bring your offering of the cattle, even of the herd, and of the flock [Lev. 1:2].

"If any man" means "whosoever will may come."

If his offering be a burnt sacrifice of the herd, let him offer a male without blemish: he shall offer it of his own voluntary will at the door of the tabernacle of the congregation before the LORD [Lev. 1:3].

"He shall offer it of his own voluntary will." May I say, this is free will with a vengeance. The Lord Jesus said, "If any man thirst, let him come. . . ." This is an all-inclusive invitation to the human family. None are excluded except those who exclude themselves. The Lord Jesus gives only one condition, "If any man thirst." You may say, "I don't thirst." Well, then maybe this isn't for you. But if you do thirst, He asks you to come to Him. He can satisfy you. Isaiah included this in his invitation, "Ho, every one that thirsteth, come yᴇ to the waters . . ." (Isa. 55:1). Anyone can come to Christ if he chooses to come. There must be a need and a desire. If you have that, come!

Two types of animals were used for the burnt offering. Animals of the herd are cattle and of the flock are sheep. Wild animals that were animals of prey were excluded. Carnivorous animals were forbidden in all sacrifices. Animals that live by slaying other animals could never reveal Christ, who came to give His life a ransom for many.

A further restriction was that the animal must be a clean animal and it must be domesticated. It could not be taken in the hunt. Only that which was valuable and dear to the owner could be offered because it prefigures Christ. God spared not His own Son. Christ suffered on the Cross, but the Father suffered in heaven. The final restriction reveals that the animal was one that was obedient to man. My, what a picture this is! Christ was the obedient servant. He came to minister and He was obedient unto death.

The burnt offering is the offering that is mentioned up to the time of Leviticus and it was the only offering that was made by those who wanted an approach to God. The burnt sacrifice is called *olah* in the Hebrew. It means "that which ascends." It is not irreverent to say that the burnt sacrifice went up in smoke. It was wholly consumed on the altar; nothing remained but the ashes. This reveals that the burnt offering is what God sees in Christ. Paul said in Ephesians 5:2 that Christ gave Himself ". . . an offering and a sacrifice to God for a sweet-smelling savour." Here in Leviticus 1 we find in verses 9, 13, and 17 that the sacrifice is "a sweet savour unto the LORD." This is what God sees in Christ. It may not be what you see in Him or what I see in Him. It is what God sees in Him, and that is the thing that is all-important. God is saying that He is satisfied with what Jesus did for your sins and for my sins. God is satisfied that Jesus has paid it all for you and that He can save you to the uttermost if you will put your trust in Him. The question is, "Are you satisfied with that?"

You will notice that it says the sacrifice is to be a male, and that speaks of strength. It speaks of the fact that the Lord Jesus is mighty to save, and that He is able to save to the uttermost (Heb. 7:25). Then, the sacrifice was to be without blemish which means the animal was to be ideally perfect. This speaks of the perfections of Christ. ". . . In him is no sin" (1 John 3:5). "Who did no sin . . ." (1 Pet. 2:22). ". . . Who knew no sin . . ." (2 Cor. 5:21). "Who is holy, harmless, undefiled, separate from sinners . . ." (Heb. 7:26). He is the beloved Son of whom the Father could say, ". . . I am well pleased" (Matt. 3:17).

He shall offer it of his own "voluntary will" is translated "that he may be accepted before Jehovah" in the American Standard Version of 1901. Because of the atoning death of the little animal, the sinner was received by God. The animal had to be offered, not in life, but in death. This was absolutely imperative. It is not the spotless life of Christ and our approval of Him that saves us. Only His death can save the sinner.

In the Gospels we find that when He died, the veil of the temple was torn in two. It was His death which opened the way to God; it was His death which saves the sinner. You see, the veil represents His flesh (Heb. 10:20). His perfect life shuts us out from God. What God demands is a life that is perfect like the life of Christ, and you and I can't reproduce it. His life is the standard. The Father could say concerning Jesus, ". . . This is my beloved Son, in whom I am well pleased" (Matt 3:17). You and I just can't measure up to that. The life of Christ therefore cannot save us. It shuts us out from God, just as the veil shut man out from God in the tabernacle. We must have another basis on which we can come to God. That way is through the death of Christ. That is what tore the veil. The minute you and I come through the death of Christ, the way to God is open. It is the death of Christ that saves the sinner.

The offering was to be brought of his own voluntary will You don't have to come to Christ. But if you want to be saved, then you will have to come to Christ. God has no other way. The Lord Jesus said, ". . . no man cometh unto the Father, but by me" (John 14:6). You may think that is dogmatic and narrow. I'll tell you something—it is! But the interesting thing is that it will bring you to God. Now, you don't have to come; that is where your free will enters in. You do not have to come, but, if you want to come to God, then you must come this one way because God has elected that this is the only way! You cannot come to God on the basis of your own "righteousness." He cannot accept your righteousness; He won't have any of it. "Not by works of righteousness which we have done, but according to his mercy he saved us . . ." (Titus 3:5).

"At the door of the tabernacle" is another imperative They

couldn't offer the sacrifice anywhere else. This was to keep Israel from idolatry. They were prone to lapse into idolatry again and again, and finally their idolatry was the reason for the Babylonian captivity. And this, by the way, has a message for us. It is to keep us from presuming that we can come to God our way, on our terms We do not make the terms by which we come to God. God makes the terms, my friend. "But we are all as an unclean thing, and all our righteousnesses are as filthy rags . . ." (Isa. 64:6). God won't accept our righteousness. A great many people think that the righteousness of God is just a projection, on a little higher level, of the righteousness of man. Nothing of the kind! It is altogether holy! The *only* righteousness which God can accept is the righteousness of God which is through faith in Christ. You can't work for it. You can't buy it. God cannot accept our poor righteousness—it will simply go down the drain. The offering must be at the door of the tabernacle. Friends, there is no other way to come to God but His way. The Lord Jesus said, "No man cometh unto the Father, but by me" (John 14:6).

And he shall put his hand upon the head of the burnt offering; and it shall be accepted for him to make atonement for him [Lev. 1:4].

"He shall put his hand upon the head of the burnt offering." Dr. Kellogg calls this "an act of designation." This is revealed in Leviticus 24:14 where the witnesses were to lay their hands on the blasphemer before he was stoned to death. Moses laid his hands on Joshua, designating him as his successor. Dr. Kellogg wrote a very fine book on Leviticus, which may be out of print now, but I would suggest you buy one if you can find it in a secondhand bookstore. Here is a quotation from it. He is speaking of the laying on of the hand upon the head of the animal, and he says, "It symbolized a transfer, according to God's merciful provision, of an obligation to suffer for sin, from the offerer to the innocent victim. Henceforth, the victim stood in the offerer's place, and was dealt with accordingly."

In other words, when the man went in and put his hand on the head of the little animal that was to be slain, he was designating this little animal to take his place. The man was confessing that he deserved to die. Friends, when you take Christ as your Savior, you are saying that you are a sinner and that you can't save yourself. You want to turn from your sins and you want to turn to the Savior and you want to live for Him. The little animal was dying a substitutionary death in the place of the offerer. That is what Christ did for us. When you accept Christ, you put your hand on Him; that is, you designate Him as your Savior.

People today seem to have the idea that there is some merit in the act of laying on of hands. They think there is some transfer of power. The only thing that can be transferred by laying on of hands is disease germs. But it does designate someone who is taking your place. When we as church leaders place our hands on a missionary, as the church in Antioch did to Paul and Barnabas, we are designating that one to go out in our place and as our representative.

Christ took our place. This is what it means when it says, ". . . He hath made him to be sin for us . . ." (2 Cor. 5:21) and "Who was delivered for our offences . . ." (Rom. 4:25).

The Hebrew here means to lay the hand so as to lean heavily upon another. "Thy wrath lieth hard upon me . . ." (Ps. 88:7). This part of the ceremony speaks of atonement and acceptance through the death of the victim—"it shall be accepted for him to make atonement for him."

We have said before that atonement means to cover, not to remove "For it is not possible that the blood of bulls and of goats should take away sins" (Heb. 10:4). Only the Lamb of God can remove sin.

This offering was done publicly. He went down to the tabernacle, he walked to the side of the altar, and there he slew the little animal. It was a public act. A sinner needs to confess Christ publicly. By faith, we place our hand on Christ, but the public needs to know that we do it. I think this is primarily the meaning of baptism today. Baptism means "to be identified with." This is a public confession of being identified with Christ in His death and in His resurrection. This is the reason water baptism was so important in the early church

THE RITUAL FOR THE BURNT SACRIFICE

And he shall kill the bullock before the Lord: and the priests, Aaron's sons, shall bring the blood, and sprinkle the blood round about upon the altar that is by the door of the tabernacle of the congregation [Lev. 1:5].

Now we come to the ritual for the burnt offering. A proper offering having been chosen—that is, the right kind of animal—the sinner brings the victim to the entrance of the tabernacle where he is met by a priest. The sinner himself slays the victim. (There is an exception in verses 14, 15.) "For the wages of sin is death . . ." (Rom. 6:23). Here the innocent dies for the guilty. Just so, "Christ also hath once suffered for sins, the just for the unjust . . ." (1 Pet. 3:18).

Our sins put Jesus Christ to death. If you want it made very personal, my sin is responsible for the death of Christ; your sin is responsible for the death of Christ. I get a little weary of hearing people argue about who is responsible for the death of Christ. They indict the religious rulers, the nation Israel, or the Roman nation. My friend, people can argue all they wish; the fact is that if I hadn't been a sinner and if you hadn't been a sinner, nobody would have put Him to death. It was our sin that put Him to death!

Every sacrifice had to be slain. Either the sinner or the priest acting for the nation slew the victim. There was no forgiveness apart from the shed blood of the victim. So today, only the blood of Christ can cleanse us from all sin. After the slaying of the victim, the priest took over by sprinkling the blood about the altar. The blood represented life and the sprinkling presented it to God.

And he shall flay the burnt offering, and cut it into his pieces.

And the sons of Aaron the priest shall put fire upon the altar, and lay the wood in order upon the fire:

And the priests, Aaron's sons, shall lay the parts, the
head, and the fat, in order upon the wood that is on the
fire which is upon the altar·

But his inwards and his legs shall he wash in water: and
the priest shall burn all on the altar, to be a burnt sacrifice, an offering made by fire, of a sweet savour unto the
LORD [Lev. 1:6–9].

Everything had to be done decently and in order. God is not the author
of confusion. The offering was to be cut into pieces so that it might be
exposed and so it could be more easily consumed by the fire. The
inner life of the Lord Jesus has been open for inspection for over 1900
years. He has been examined more than any other person. There is
more disagreement concerning Him than anyone else. This was true
at the time He lived and it is still true today. He still asks the question,
"Whom do men say that I the Son of man am?" There are all kinds of
opinions today and some of them are blasphemous. Yet it is still true
that He is "holy, harmless, undefiled, separate from sinners." Jesus
Christ, who has been under examination all these years, is still the
One who is altogether lovely.

And if his offering be of the flocks, namely, of the sheep,
or of the goats, for a burnt sacrifice; he shall bring it a
male without blemish.

And he shall kill it on the side of the altar northward
before the LORD: and the priests, Aaron's sons, shall
sprinkle his blood round about upon the altar.

And he shall cut it into his pieces, with his head and his
fat: and the priest shall lay them in order on the wood
that is on the fire which is upon the altar:

But he shall wash the inwards and the legs with water:
and the priest shall bring it all, and burn it upon the
altar: it is a burnt sacrifice, an offering made by fire, of a
sweet savour unto the LORD [Lev. 1:10–13].

Notice again, the offer is cut in pieces and totally exposed.

Fire was to be used on the altar. The fire does not necessarily represent hell, vengeance, or wrath. I disagree with those who magnify that so much. Fire did not represent that at the burning bush. Fire oftentimes represents the purifying energy and the resistless power of God. "And he shall sit as a refiner and purifier of silver: and he shall purify the sons of Levi, and purge them as gold and silver . . ." (Mal. 3:3). Fire is that resistless energy of God which sometimes destroys and sometimes cleanses and sometimes consumes. The *nature of the object* determines the process it will take.

Here in the burnt offering, it speaks of the total commitment of Christ to God. It is absolute consecration. In our experience this is essential also, if we are to worship God in spirit and in truth. "For the LORD thy God is a consuming fire, even a jealous God" (Deut. 4:24).

My friend, you cannot just play around and get very far with God. That is the reason there is so much that is phony in Christian service today. I want to say it kindly but emphatically—you are not serving God unless you are letting Him cleanse and purify your life. We have forgotten this matter of holiness today. How we need it in our churches and in our own lives!

> **And if the burnt sacrifice for his offering to the LORD be of fowls, then he shall bring his offering of turtledoves, or of young pigeons.**

> **And the priest shall bring it unto the altar, and wring off his head, and burn it on the altar; and the blood thereof shall be wrung out at the side of the altar:**

> **And he shall pluck away his crop with his feathers, and cast it beside the altar on the east part, by the place of the ashes [Lev. 1:14–16].**

Poverty was no excuse for not bringing an offering to God. A bird could be substituted for an animal. Anyone could have a bird and offer it. Did you notice that when our Lord was born, His parents offered turtledoves? His parents were poor and He was born in poverty

THE REASON FOR THE BURNT SACRIFICE

And he shall cleave it with the wings thereof, but shall not divide it asunder: and the priest shall burn it upon the altar, upon the wood that is upon the fire: it is a burnt sacrifice, an offering made by fire, of a sweet savour unto the LORD [Lev. 1:17].

This is the third time it is mentioned that it is a sweet savor to the Lord. This makes it clear that this was the reason for the sacrifice. It is what God sees in Jesus Christ.

THE LAW OF THE BURNT SACRIFICE

The law of the burnt offering is found in Leviticus 6:8–13. The morning and the evening offerings were burnt sacrifices offered by Aaron and the priests for the nation to God (Exod. 29:38–46). It was called the *continual* burnt offering. Christ in consecration *ever* lives to make intercession for us. This is most beautifully expressed in an ancient "Order for the Visitation of the Sick," attributed to Anselm of Canterbury:

The minister shall say to the sick man: Dost thou believe that thou canst not be saved but by the death of Christ? The sick man answereth, Yes. Then let it be said unto him: Go to, then, and whilst thy soul abideth in thee, put all thy confidence in this death alone; place thy trust in no other thing; commit thyself wholly to this death; cover thyself wholly with this alone . . . And if God would judge thee, say: Lord! I place the death of our Lord Jesus Christ between me and Thy judgment; otherwise I will not contend or enter into judgment with Thee.

And if He shall say unto thee that thou art a sinner, say: I place the death of our Lord Jesus Christ between me and my sins. If He shall say unto thee, that thou hast deserved damnation, say: Lord! I put the death of our Lord Jesus Christ between Thee and all my sins; and I offer His merits for my own, which I should have, and have not.

And whosoever of us can thus speak, to him the promise speaks from out the shadows of the tent of meeting: "This Christ, the Lamb of God, the true burnt offering, shall be accepted for thee, to make atonement for thee!"

This is the law of the burnt offering. God is satisfied with Jesus and He sees us in Christ. He is satisfied, then, with us. "But now the righteousness of God without the law is manifested, being witnessed by the law and the prophets; even the righteousness of God which is by faith of Jesus Christ unto all and upon all them that believe: for there is no difference: for all have sinned, and come short of the glory of God; being justified freely by his grace through the redemption that is in Christ Jesus" (Rom. 3:21–24).

My friend, do you have the sacrifice of Christ between you and your sins? Has His blood been shed that you might live? Have you trusted Him today? God sees Christ as the only One who can satisfy Him for your sins. Have you seen Him like that? Are you still trying to bring your little puny self and your little goodness to offer to God? God won't take that. He only accepts what Christ has done for you and He counts the righteousness of Christ as your righteousness. Trust Him today and live!

CHAPTER 2

THEME: *Offerings mixed but unbaked; offerings mixed and baked; offering of firstfruits; the law of the meal offering*

The offerings speak of the person of Christ and of the work of Christ. The burnt offering was a picture of Christ in depth as well as in death. The meal offering reveals the humanity of Jesus in all its perfection and loveliness.

As you read this, you will see it is like a recipe for bread. That is exactly what it is. It is really the *meal* offering. The Authorized Version calls it a meat offering, which is a misleading term for us today, as no meat was connected with it at all. There is no shedding of blood; so this offering was different from the others. However, it was generally offered with some offering in which there was the shedding of blood. This meal offering could be offered either baked or unbaked. Aaron and his sons received a portion of this offering for themselves. It was to be eaten by all the males in the family of Aaron.

The meal or food offering sets forth the humanity of Jesus in all His perfections. His deity is not in view here. He was perfectly human, and He was the perfect human. God's goal for man is fulfilled in Jesus. He is the second man, but the last Adam. There will be no more Adams, but there will be some more men who are made just like Him. He is the last Adam, the Head of a new people. "Beloved, now are we the sons of God, and it doth not yet appear what we shall be: but we know that, when he shall appear, we shall be like him; for we shall see him as he is" (1 John 3:2).

Friends, man as he is in the world today is the most colossal failure in God's universe. Have you ever stopped to think about that? The Scriptures are outspoken and specific at this point. "They are all gone out of the way, [the original here suggests that they are a wreck] they are together become unprofitable . . ." and ". . . all have sinned, and come short of the glory of God" (Rom. 3:12, 23).

God cannot save us on the basis of our keeping His Law for the very simple reason that God sees our imperfections. We cannot fulfill or keep the Law. We cannot render perfection to Him. God can't save us in our imperfections because He is a holy God and demands absolute righteousness and perfection. Imperfection is the very best that we can do. Therefore, mankind is a failure.

"The way of peace they have not known" is confirmed in every morning newspaper. Why is this? Because war and violence are in the very heart of man. It is almost amusing to hear about the peace demonstrations that end up in a *brawl!* With feverish energy man is presently trying to perfect fiendish instruments of frightful destruction. Surely this is not the goal of man!

God has another purpose in view for man and if you want to see what He has in mind, look at Jesus. Here is the Man who pleased God. There was a glory in His manhood. The loveliness of Jesus was truly a sweet perfume. His coming was a doxology; His stay was a blessing; His departure was a benediction. His winsomeness has filled the world with a new hope and ideal concerning man.

There are two important aspects of this offering: the ingredients which are included and the ingredients which are excluded.

OFFERINGS MIXED BUT UNBAKED

And when any will offer a meat offering unto the Lord, his offering shall be of fine flour; and he shall pour oil upon it, and put frankincense thereon [Lev. 2:1].

The offering was to be made of fine flour and fine flour in that day was a little unusual. They didn't have the great mills as we have today in Minneapolis. Actually, they ground it by hand in a kind of rock bowl. They used a pestle, with which they just beat the grain down. It was often very coarse and uneven if the grinder was careless or in a hurry. If the flour was to be very fine, it meant they must spend a great deal of time with it. This offering had to be made of very fine flour which means that it was well beaten.

This sets before us the Lord Jesus in His personality. Today I am sure we would use the expression that He had a well-integrated personality. He was a normal person. Actually, I think He was the only normal person who has ever been on this earth. Sin has made all of the human race lumpy, one-sided, abnormal. One part of our personality has overdeveloped at the expense of some other area of our personality.

In college I studied abnormal psychology. In my last year of college I went to see the professor of the department and said that I needed to talk to him. I told him that when we looked at the etiology of the disease of every form of abnormality that we had been studying, I found that I had symptoms of all these forms of abnormality. He broke out in laughter and said to me, "I was wondering when you would come. All the rest of the class has been here. They all have it, and I have it, too." You see, all of us do. Recently a leading psychologist made the statement that all of mankind today is a little "off." We are all just a little off-center. Jesus was the only normal person.

Notice how uneven were the characters of men of the Bible. Samson was enabled to perform great physical feats, but he seems to have been weak both in will and mind. In fact, he was a sissy. Paul was a mental giant, but he appeared to be weak in body. Simon Peter was moved by his emotions, even declaring that he would die for Jesus, yet he denied Him, which reveals a definite weakness in the area of the volition. King Saul was self-willed and stubborn, unable to bow the knee in obedience to God. This led to his dismissal and then to his death. All of these men were lumpy. They had over and underdeveloped personalities.

In contrast to them and all of us, Jesus was well balanced. He had equal poise in all areas of His personality. He could drive the money changers from the temple, and He could take the little children into His arms. When He was twelve years old, the religious rulers marvelled at His wisdom. When He began to teach, the people were amazed, saying, ". . . How knoweth this man letters, having never learned?" (John 7:15). Nevertheless, the Lord Jesus never appealed to

His intellect as the basis for any judgment. Have you ever noticed that this was never the criterion for His conduct? He came to do the Father's will, and that was the motive for His actions.

Jesus could weep at the tomb of Lazarus or over the indifferent city of Jerusalem. At the same time, He would raise Lazarus from the dead, and He would pronounce a severe judgment on Jerusalem (which was literally fulfilled). He wasn't swayed or guided by His emotions. He was never self-willed, yet nothing could hinder Him from going to Jerusalem to die. At all times He could say, "Not as I will, but as thou wilt." "For I came down from heaven, not to do mine own will, but the will of him that sent me" (John 6:38). His own volitional nature was not the guideline for His action. He was even; all of us are lumpy.

"He shall pour oil upon it"—olive oil speaks of the Holy Spirit. You will notice that here it is "oil upon it." In verses 4 and 5 it is "mingled with oil"; in verse 6 it is "pour oil thereon"; in verse 7 it is "with oil." The offering was drenched with oil. The oil was a very important part of the offering and was applied in many different ways.

The prominence of the Holy Spirit in the human life of Jesus is very noticeable. He was born of the Spirit—"mingled with oil" (Luke 1:35). He was baptized of the Spirit—"oil upon it" (Matt. 3:16–17). He was led of the Spirit—"pour oil thereon" (Mark 1:12). He taught, performed miracles, and offered Himself in the power of the Holy Spirit—"with oil" (John 3:34; Matt. 12:28).

If the Lord Jesus in His perfect humanity needed the Holy Spirit, surely you and I need Him to an even greater extent. We can do nothing of ourselves.

Frankincense was made from a secret formula. There evidently was a form of incense with which it was mixed (Exod. 30:34), but was distinguished from it. It was made from some part of a plant or tree, perhaps the bark or leaves, and it exuded its fragrance only when crushed, beaten, burned, or put under pressure. This speaks of the life of the Lord Jesus as He manifested the fragrance of His life under the fires of tension, pressures, and persecution. This is what the Father saw in Him as the One in whom He delighted. There was a special fragrance about His life, and there should be a fragrance in our lives also, since we belong to Him.

> And he shall bring it to Aaron's sons the priests: and he shall take thereout his handful of the flour thereof, and of the oil thereof, with all the frankincense thereof; and the priest shall burn the memorial of it upon the altar, to be an offering made by fire, of a sweet savour unto the Lord [Lev. 2:2].

The priests received a portion of the meal offering. They were to take out a percentage of each item. Apparently the remainder was mixed and then burnt upon the altar.

> And the remnant of the meat offerings shall be Aaron's and his sons': it is a thing most holy of the offerings of the Lord made by fire [Lev. 2:3].

Emphasis is laid upon the fact that this offering was burnt upon the altar although no blood was shed in connection with it. Great emphasis is placed upon the fire (verses 2, 9, 16 and chapter 6:15, 17–18).

OFFERINGS MIXED AND BAKED

> And if thou bring an oblation of a meat offering baken in the oven, it shall be unleavened cakes of fine flour mingled with oil, or unleavened wafers anointed with oil.

> And if thy oblation be a meat offering baken in a pan, it shall be of fine flour unleavened, mingled with oil.

> Thou shalt part it in pieces, and pour oil thereon: it is a meat offering.

> And if thy oblation be a meat offering baken in the fryingpan, it shall be made of fine flour with oil.

> And thou shalt bring the meat offering that is made of these things unto the Lord: and when it is presented unto the priest, he shall bring it unto the altar.

And the priest shall take from the meat offering a memorial thereof, and shall burn it upon the altar: it is an offering made by fire, of a sweet savour unto the LORD.

And that which is left of the meat offering shall be Aaron's and his sons': it is a thing most holy of the offerings of the LORD made by fire [Lev. 2:4–10].

These are detailed instructions for the ritual of the meal offering and it sounds, very frankly, like a recipe for making bread. The emphasis upon the fine flour and the oil is repeated again and again. Also, the fire is mentioned over and over. I want to say with great emphasis that the fire here does not symbolize hell under any circumstance. It is God's purifying energy and power which brought out the sweetness in the life of Christ.

In verse 9 it is specifically declared to be a "sweet savour unto the Lord." The final and full meaning of this offering is what God sees in Christ. His sweetness came out under pressure. In your experience and mine sweetness doesn't always come out from us when we are under pressure. I've heard some Christians say some very ugly things when they were under tension. But as more tension was placed on Him, the sweeter He was. The Lord Jesus could say, "And he that sent me is with me: the Father hath not left me alone; for I do always those things that please him" (John 8:29).

What was left of the meal offering was to be Aaron's and his sons'. Believers have the high privilege of sharing Christ with God the Father. What do you see in Him? Is there sweetness about Him? Have you smelled the sweetness and fragrance of His life?

"Then Jesus said unto them, Verily, verily, I say unto you, Except ye eat the flesh of the Son of man, and drink his blood, ye have no life in you. Whoso eateth my flesh, and drinketh my blood, hath eternal life; and I will raise him up at the last day. For my flesh is meat indeed, and my blood is drink indeed. He that eateth my flesh, and drinketh my blood, dwelleth in me, and I in him. As the living Father hath sent me, and I live by the Father: so he that eateth me, even he shall live by me. This is that bread which came down from heaven: not as your fathers did eat manna, and are dead: he that eateth of this bread shall live for ever" (John 6:53–58). If you want any sweetness in your life, and if I want any, we must partake of Christ. Not literally, of course. We are not cannibals. We partake of Him by faith and we appropriate Him into our lives. As we partake of Him, the sweetness of His life should come into our lives.

> **No meat offering, which ye shall bring unto the Lord, shall be made with leaven: for ye shall burn no leaven, nor any honey, in any offering of the Lord made by fire [Lev. 2:11].**

The ingredients excluded in this offering are as prominent as the ingredients included. The two mentioned here by name are leaven and honey.

Leaven will be mentioned in the Scriptures again and again. Leaven in Scripture is everywhere presented as a principle of evil. The Lord Jesus Christ warned His disciples of the leaven of the Pharisees. He was talking about the doctrine of the Pharisees, their teaching. That is the leaven. Evil teaching is the leaven. Leaven is the principle of evil. Leaven is to be excluded from the offering. This speaks of the fact that there is no evil in Christ. There is no sin in the life of Christ.

Honey was also excluded. It represents natural sweetness. It will sour, just as leaven is a souring thing. There are Christians who assume a pious pose in public. They wear a Sunday smile. They call everyone "brother" and "my dear So-and-So." Their halo is polished with the latest miracle cleanser. Yet these same folk can and do engage in vicious slander and malicious gossip. They are more dangerous than a killer with a gun. May I say to you that there are a lot of folk who have honey in their lives.

The Lord Jesus told it like it is, friends. There was no corrupting principle in the life of Jesus. He did not exhibit honey sweetness, nor was there any leaven in His speech that made it acceptable to the natural man.

> As for the oblation of the firstfruits, ye shall offer them
> unto the LORD: but they shall not be burnt on the altar for
> a sweet savour [Lev. 2:12].

This offering was a sweet savor sacrifice, but it was not to derive its
sweetness from the palatable ingredient of leaven nor the natural
sweetness of honey.

> And every oblation of thy meat offering shalt thou sea-
> son with salt; neither shalt thou suffer the salt of the cov-
> enant of thy God to be lacking from thy meat offering:
> with all thine offerings thou shalt offer salt [Lev. 2:13].

Salt is the final ingredient which was included in the meal offering.
Salt is a preservative and is the opposite of leaven. Leaven produces
decay; salt preserves from corruption. "The salt of the covenant" is
still eaten among Arabs as a seal to bind one in faithful obedience to a
covenant.

Salt was the token of faithfulness between the offerer and God.
Christ is faithful. This is one of His many-faceted names. He is Faithful and True (Rev. 19:11). He is the Lord Jesus.

Christ offered Himself to God. We can offer ourselves to God because of His mercy. We ought to be found faithful. Christians are to be
the salt in the world. We do this by offering ourselves as a living sacrifice to God (Rom. 12:1–2).

OFFERING OF FIRSTFRUITS

> And if thou offer a meat offering of thy firstfruits unto
> the LORD, thou shalt offer for the meat offering of thy
> firstfruits green ears of corn dried by the fire, even corn
> beaten out of full ears.

> And thou shalt put oil upon it, and lay frankincense
> thereon: it is a meat offering.

> And the priest shall burn the memorial of it, part of the beaten corn thereof, and part of the oil thereof, with all the frankincense thereof: it is an offering made by fire unto the LORD [Lev. 2:14–16].

The Feast of Firstfruits, as given in Leviticus 23:9–14, was a meal offering as well as the Feast of Pentecost.

THE LAW OF THE MEAL OFFERING

The law of the meal offering is given in Leviticus 6:14–23. It reveals that with every burnt sacrifice in the morning and in the evening, a meal offering was also made. (See Exod. 29:39–40.)

The meal offering sets forth Christ in His consecration. It also represents the consecration of believers in Christ. It pictures the perfect humanity of Christ.

CHAPTER 3

THEME: *A sacrifice from the herd; a sacrifice from the flock; a sacrifice from the goats; the law of the peace offering*

This offering speaks of the communion and fellowship of believers with God the Father through our Lord Jesus Christ. The only way you and I can come to God is through Jesus Christ. He is the Way!

No single offering can set forth the manifold wonders of the person of Christ and the many facets of His glory. Just as we need four Gospels in the New Testament to set forth His earthly life, so also we need the five offerings of Leviticus to set forth His person and work.

We will notice that there are striking similarities between the peace offering and the burnt offering, but we will also note sharp contrast. So the peace offering is also a unique offering.

The peace offering does not speak of the peace that Christ made through His blood on the Cross, as that has to do with sin and comes properly under the non-sweet savor offerings. It is concerning Christ being made our Peace as regards sin that Paul writes in Colossians 1:20–22: "And, having made peace through the blood of his cross, by him to reconcile all things unto himself; by him, I say, whether they be things in earth, or things in heaven. And you, that were sometime alienated and enemies in your mind by wicked works, yet now hath he reconciled in the body of his flesh through death, to present you holy and unblameable and unreproveable in his sight." That is not the peace offering.

Rather, the peace offering speaks more specifically of the peace to which Paul referred in Ephesians, the peace which brings all believers into communion with the Father by the Holy Spirit, through the Lord Jesus Christ. "But now in Christ Jesus ye who sometimes were far off are made nigh by the blood of Christ. For he is our peace, who hath made both one, and hath broken down the middle wall of partition between us; having abolished in his flesh the enmity, even the law of commandments contained in ordinances; for to make in himself of twain one new man, so making peace; and that he might reconcile both unto God in one body by the cross, having slain the enmity thereby: and came and preached peace to you which were afar off, and to them that were nigh. For through him we both have access by one Spirit unto the Father. Now therefore ye are no more strangers and foreigners, but fellow-citizens with the saints, and of the household of God; and are built upon the foundation of the apostles and prophets, Jesus Christ himself being the chief corner stone; in whom all the building fitly framed together groweth unto an holy temple in the Lord: in whom ye also are builded together for an habitation of God through the Spirit" (Eph. 2:13–22).

In the peace offering, the emphasis is not upon the peace that He made by the blood of the Cross, but upon the peace He *is* because of the blood of the Cross. He is the meeting place of all believers together and of each believer with God the Father. Christ is the only one who can break down the walls that separate individuals, families, religions, races, and nations. All are made one in Christ. Then they become a habitation of God in the Spirit and have access to the Father. You see, only believers can join together in partaking of the wonders, the beauties, and the glories of Christ. They can have communion with the Father and fellowship one with another as they share the things of Christ.

This is what the apostle John is saying. "That which we have seen and heard declare we unto you, that ye also may have fellowship with us: and truly our fellowship is with the Father, and with his Son Jesus Christ" (1 John 1:3). The peace offering brings us together. It is only as we meet around the person of Christ that we can be drawn together. Friends, don't tell me to have fellowship with every Tom, Dick, and Harry! I cannot. But there is *nothing* that keeps me from fellowshiping with any person, I don't care who he is, *if* he can meet with me around the person of Christ. We are all made one there. We are all on the same level there. We can all enjoy the person of Christ.

A SACRIFICE FROM THE HERD

And if his oblation be a sacrifice of peace offering, if he offer it of the herd; whether it be a male or female, he shall offer it without blemish before the LORD [Lev. 3:1].

The peace offering is in one sense all comprehensive. The sinner can come to God because Christ made peace by the blood of His Cross. There is also communion with God and fellowship with Him on the basis of peace by the blood of His Cross. Christ and His work of redemption is the complete satisfaction for peace. The emphasis of the peace offering, however, is chiefly on the communion.

What is the gospel appeal to the sinner? Well, it is like this. God says to you and me as sinners, "You are lost. You are alienated from Me, so I will have to consign you to the darkness of eternity." If God did that, He would be just and holy and all the angels in heaven would sing praises to His name. But, my friend, God is satisfied with what Jesus did for you and now you can come to God. The gospel message is this: "God is reconciled!" The question is, "Will you be reconciled?" God is satisfied with what Jesus did. That is the message. That is the good news. God has already turned to you. Will you turn to Him? He will accept you because of what Christ has done. Will you be satisfied with Christ and what He has done, and will you come to God and have fellowship? That is the peace that you can know.

The peace offering is different from the burnt offering in several respects. In the burnt offering only a male could be offered, but here it can be either a male or female—but without blemish. The offerer will never find as much in Christ as God finds in Him. In the burnt offering it speaks of what God sees in Christ. In the peace offering it is the offerer who finds something in Christ. The female offering was permitted because here the capacity of the offerer to enjoy Christ is in view. The offerer will never find as much in Christ as God finds in Him.

> **And he shall lay his hand upon the head of his offering, and kill it at the door of the tabernacle of the congregation: and Aaron's sons the priests shall sprinkle the blood upon the altar round about [Lev. 3:2].**

Up to this point, it duplicates the burnt offering.

> **And he shall offer of the sacrifice of the peace offering an offering made by fire unto the LORD; the fat that cov-**

> ereth the inwards, and all the fat that is upon the in-
> wards.
>
> And the two kidneys, and the fat that is on them, which
> is by the flanks, and the caul above the liver, with the
> kidneys, it shall he take away [Lev. 3:3–4].

Here the contrast with the burnt sacrifice is noted. *All* of the burnt offering was placed on that altar. In the peace offering, only a portion was offered. The portion was specified. It was to be the choice portion which included the fat and the inward parts. These speak of the hidden riches, the precious qualities, the priceless value of the character of Christ that God alone knows.

Sometimes a loved one knows the real worth of a great man who has been bitterly assailed in public. Early in my ministry, I became acquainted with a great preacher, and he and his family became my friends. An attack was made upon him, and harsh things were said about him. His family knew and I knew that they were lies. Just so, there are a lot of things said about Christ that are not true. A great many people say, "I don't understand this and I don't understand that about Christ." There is a lot I don't understand about Him either. But God knows Him! God sees more in Him than you and I can see. God sees the inward parts. We just don't know Him. That is why Paul cried out, "That I may know him, and the power of his resurrection, and the fellowship of his sufferings . . ." (Phil. 3:10).

> And Aaron's sons shall burn it on the altar upon the
> burnt sacrifice, which is upon the wood that is on the
> fire: it is an offering made by fire, of a sweet savour unto
> the LORD [Lev. 3:5].

The offering was consumed by fire and this speaks of the total dedication of Christ and His human testing and sufferings. It is specifically labeled, "a sweet savour unto the LORD." The emphasis is still upon the person of Christ and not upon His work. It is His perfect life that is in view, not His death for sin. His sufferings in life were not for the sins of the world. Even in the first three hours on the Cross, His suffering was at the hands of men. It was during the last three hours on the

Cross that it became an altar on which the Son of God was offered. Darkness veiled from the eye of man those last three hours when it pleased the Lord to bruise Him, when He put Him to grief, when He made His soul an offering for sin (Isa. 53:10).

Notice that the peace offering was put together with the burnt offering. They belong together in order to get the full view of the inward values and glories of Christ.

A SACRIFICE FROM THE FLOCK

And if his offering for a sacrifice of peace offering unto the LORD be of the flock; male or female, he shall offer it without blemish.

If he offer a lamb for his offering, then shall he offer it before the LORD [Lev. 3:6–7].

The lamb sets forth in a peculiar way the character of Christ and is, therefore, unusually appropriate as a sacrifice in the peace offering.

By contrast the bullock, or the heifer from the herd, sets forth the servant side of our Lord's ministry. The bullock was a domesticated animal, used to bear burdens and to plow fields, and so represented transportation and commerce in that day. The bullock was a servant and a friend of man. The bullock represents Christ as a servant. This is the aspect of Christ's ministry which is set forth in the Gospel of Mark. We need to emphasize that Christ as a servant was not a bellboy or a shoeshiner for man. He did not run at man's bidding. The Gospel of Mark sets Him forth as *God's* Servant. He came to do the will of God.

However, the *lamb* sets forth Christ in His complete identification with man in life and in death. Have you ever noticed that? At the beginning of His ministry, John the Baptist pointed Him out as ". . . the Lamb of God, which taketh away the sin of the world" (John 1:29). That referred to His work. Later, he said, ". . . Behold the Lamb of God!" (John 1:36)—referring to His person.

From the beginning, the Lamb has set forth His quality and ability to take the place of man in bearing the sin of the world. The very first offering made by Abel was the sacrifice of a lamb. I think that God clothed Adam and Eve with lambs' skins. I can't prove that, but I believe it in view of the fact that Abel brought a lamb.

Isaiah 53 makes it very clear that Jesus Christ was our substitute, carrying our sins and iniquities. ". . . He is brought as a lamb to the slaughter, and as a sheep before her shearers is dumb, so he openeth not his mouth" (Isa. 53:7). He is pictured as a lamb. The Lamb becomes our substitute.

He is also called a lamb in His resurrection. "And I beheld, and, lo, in the midst of the throne and of the four beasts, and in the midst of the elders, stood a Lamb as it had been slain, having seven horns and seven eyes, which are the seven Spirits of God sent forth into all the earth" (Rev. 5:6). Again, He is a Lamb in His return in glory. "And said to the mountains and rocks, Fall on us, and hide us from the face of him that sitteth on the throne, and from the wrath of the Lamb: for the great day of his wrath is come; and who shall be able to stand?" (Rev. 6:16–17).

The lamb is probably the most complete representation of Christ of all the sacrifices.

> **And he shall lay his hand upon the head of his offering, and kill it before the tabernacle of the congregation: and Aaron's sons shall sprinkle the blood thereof round about upon the altar.**
>
> **And he shall offer of the sacrifice of the peace offering an offering made by fire unto the LORD; the fat thereof, and the whole rump, it shall he take off hard by the backbone; and the fat that covereth the inwards, and all the fat that is upon the inwards.**
>
> **And the two kidneys, and the fat that is upon them, which is by the flanks, and the caul above the liver, with the kidneys, it shall he take away [Lev. 3:8–10].**

The ritual is similar to that given concerning one of the herd. The fat was God's portion. It was considered the better part of the animal. A fat animal was the best type, and the best was offered to God.

There are many passages to illustrate that fat was considered the best: ". . . Go your way, eat the fat, and drink the sweet . . ." (Neh. 8:10). "And in this mountain shall the LORD of hosts make unto all people a feast of fat things, a feast of wines on the lees, of fat things full of marrow, of wines on the lees well refined" (Isa. 25:6). "And bring hither the fatted calf, and kill it; and let us eat, and be merry" (Luke 15:23). Today, those of us who need to reduce our weight try not to eat the fat, but it is obvious that the fat was considered the choice part. God precisely declared, "all the fat that is upon the inwards and the two kidneys and the fat that is upon them" was to be for Him. God demanded the best.

We see here the deep and full meaning of the peace offering. Fellowship with God rests upon the blood of Christ, it is true, but there is another aspect of this fellowship. To make it complete and final there must be the presentation of the life of the believer in total dedication. Both of these aspects are included by Jesus Christ in His wonderful, inclusive invitation: "Come unto me, all ye that labour and are heavy laden, and I will give you rest" (Matt. 11:28). There is a rest that He gives, which is typified by the shed blood. This is the rest of redemption. "Take my yoke upon you, and learn of me; for I am meek and lowly in heart: and ye shall find rest unto your souls. For my yoke is easy, and my burden is light" (Matt. 11:29–30)—this is a rest that we find, which is represented by the fat. We must come to Him and offer ourselves to Him. This is the rest of dedication.

The expression "the whole rump" is translated in the American Standard Version of 1901 as "the fat tail entire." This has reference to a special breed of sheep peculiar to that geographical area. The tail of this breed weighs as much as 15 pounds, and is very fatty.

And the priest shall burn it upon the altar: it is the food of the offering made by fire unto the LORD [Lev. 3:11].

This is a strange clause and some have tried to associate it with pagan offerings. We know from an Assyrian inscription of Esarhaddon that offerers sacrificed victims to the gods and then feasted with the gods. However, in the peace offering, the very opposite is true. God feasts the offerer. God makes this very clear in Deuteronomy 12:6-7: "And thither ye shall bring your burnt offerings, and your sacrifices, and your tithes, and heave offerings of your hand, and your vows, and your freewill offerings, and the firstlings of your herds and of your flocks: and there ye shall eat before the LORD your God, and ye shall rejoice in all that ye put your hand unto, ye and your households, wherein the LORD thy God hath blessed thee." The fat was totally consumed, but the priest received the breast and the shoulder. The offerer ate the remainder, and he did it in God's house. God was the host and the offerer, the sinner was the guest.

Heathenism has it backwards and that was the basis of Isaiah's charge against Israel when they went into idolatry. "But ye are they that forsake the LORD, that forget my holy mountain, that prepare a table for that troop, and that furnish the drink offering unto that number" (Isa. 65:11). The American Standard Version says, "that prepare a table for Fortune, and that fill up mingled wine unto Destiny."

God provides the table and the peace offering! This throws light upon many verses of Scripture: "Thou preparest a table before me in the presence of mine enemies . . ." (Ps. 23:5). "They shall be abundantly satisfied with the fatness of thy house . . ." (Ps. 36:8). "I am the living bread which came down from heaven: if any man eat of this bread, he shall live for ever . . . so he that eateth me, even he shall live by me" (John 6:51, 57). ". . . Take, eat; this is my body" (Matt. 26:26).

The Lord prepares the table of salvation and fellowship. This is emphasized in the peace offering. This helps us to understand the parable of the prodigal son. It is the Father who kills the fatted calf when the son is restored to fellowship. In the parable of the great supper, it is the Lord who invites, ". . . Come; for all things are now ready" (Luke 14:17). This is the table of salvation which God has provided. And then read 1 John chapter 1 again and again. Fellowship with God rests upon the redemption of Christ through His blood and upon our knowing Christ and confessing our sins. First we accept God's salvation by accepting Jesus Christ as our Savior; then we come to the table of fellowship.

Modern man thinks he can provide a table of salvation of his own works and invite God to come to eat. My friend, that is a purely pagan notion. God provides the table of salvation; God provides the table of fellowship.

A SACRIFICE FROM THE GOATS

And if his offering be a goat, then he shall offer it before the LORD [Lev. 3:12].

This is the third and final type of sacrifice for the peace offering. All three types of sacrifice are essential to portray the different aspects of Christ in the peace offering. The goat represents the complete identification of Christ as adequate to take away the sin of man. He was made sin for us. That is not just a nice statement but an actual fact. He is the propitiation for our sins, which means that He adequately and totally paid the penalty for our sins. You hear the expression, "I don't want anyone to make a goat of me." Well, friends, Christ was willing to be made a goat for you. He took the full penalty of your sin and my sin. His offering for sin is clearly set forth in Hebrews 10:6–14.

The ritual of it follows the pattern of the offering of the herd and of the flock.

And he shall lay his hand upon the head of it, and kill it before the tabernacle of the congregation: and the sons of Aaron shall sprinkle the blood thereof upon the altar round about.

And he shall offer thereof his offering, even an offering made by fire unto the LORD; the fat that covereth the inwards, and all the fat that is upon the inwards,

And the two kidneys, and the fat that is upon them, which is by the flanks, and the caul above the liver, with the kidneys, it shall he take away.

And the priest shall burn them upon the altar: it is the food of the offering made by fire for a sweet savour: all the fat is the LORD's.

It shall be a perpetual statute for your generations throughout all your dwellings, that ye eat neither fat nor blood [Lev. 3:13–17].

There are two statements here that should detain us for a moment: "all the fat is the LORD's" and "that ye eat neither fat nor blood." These two prohibitions are indeed striking. They are amplified in the law of the peace offerings in chapter 7.

The reason for the prohibition of eating blood is stated in Leviticus 17:10–14, and we will go into that later in our study.

The reason for the prohibition of eating the fat is given here. The fat is the Lord's. Man was reminded that he was redeemed by blood. That is the basis and ground of our acceptance before God. That brings us to the table of communion and fellowship with God. But the fat is the Lord's. He demands the best. If we are to enjoy to the fullest our fellowship with Him, it is imperative that we give Him our best. There must be total dedication to Him. Loving sacrifice of our lives must follow our redemption in order to enter into His sweet peace of communion. This is the message of Romans 12, John 15:14, and Philippians 3:10–14. Salvation is by the blood. Sanctification and service are by the fat.

THE LAW OF THE PEACE OFFERING

The law of the peace offering is given in Leviticus 7:11–38. It is the most extensive of all the instructions of the five offerings and it is the last. The value of the other offerings must be entered into before we can enjoy the peace of God.

We will go into more detail in chapter 7. Suffice it to say here that Aaron and his sons, the priests, received as their portion of the peace offering the breast and the shoulder. The breast speaks of the love of Christ for us and the shoulder speaks of the power and strength of Christ. He is able to save to the uttermost. This is our portion in Christ.

Do you hear Him, Christian friend, do you hear Him in His peace offering?

CHAPTER 4

THEME: Sins of ignorance; sins of the priest; sins of the congregation; sins of the ruler; sins of the common people; the law of the sin offering

This is the first of the non-sweet savor offerings. The three sweet savor offerings set forth the *person* of Christ in all of His glorious character. The two non-sweet savor offerings set forth the *work* of Christ on the Cross for sin. The sin offering speaks of sin as a nature. The trespass offering speaks of sin as an act. You see, man is a sinner by nature, and he is a sinner because of what he does. He does what he does because he is a sinner by nature.

Several striking features of the sin offering set it apart from the other offerings and distinguish its importance:

1. It is the longest account of any offering since it is twice as long as any of the other four. The burnt offering was 17 verses; the meal offering, 16 verses; the peace offering, 17 verses; the trespass offering, 19 verses; the sin offering, 35 verses. Evidently the Spirit of God thought this was very important.

2. The sin offering was an entirely new offering. Up to this time, there is no record anywhere of a sin offering. There is no previous record of it occurring in Scripture. No heathen nation had anything that was even similar to it.

3. From the time of the giving of the Law, it became the most important and significant offering. You see, man was a sinner before the giving of the Law, but actually it was the Law which revealed to him that he was a sinner. The sin offering was offered during all of the feasts—Passover, Pentecost, Trumpets, and Tabernacles. It was offered on the great Day of Atonement (Yom Kippur). It brought the High Priest into the Holy of Holies.

4. It is in contrast to the burnt sacrifice, although it was made in the same place. "Speak unto Aaron and to his sons, saying, This is the law of the sin offering: in the place where the burnt offering is killed

shall the sin offering be killed before the LORD: it is most holy" (Lev. 6:25).

Where the burnt offering leaves off, the sin offering begins. The burnt offering tells *who* Christ *is*; the sin offering tells *what* Christ *did*. In the burnt offering Christ meets the demands of God's high and holy standard; in the sin offering Christ meets the deep and desperate needs of man. In the burnt offering we see the preciousness of Christ; in the sin offering we see the hatefulness of sin.

The burnt offering was a voluntary offering; the sin offering was commanded. The burnt offering ascended; the sin offering was poured out. The one went up and the other went down.

SINS OF IGNORANCE

And the LORD spake unto Moses, saying,

Speak unto the children of Israel, saying, If a soul shall sin through ignorance against any of the commandments of the LORD concerning things which ought not to be done, and shall do against any of them [Lev. 4:1–2].

The emphasis here is upon a sin committed in ignorance. If a man sinned willfully and deliberately, this offering did not avail. "He that despised Moses' law died without mercy under two or three witnesses" (Heb. 10:28). This speaks of the fact that there is no salvation for a person who wilfully rejects Jesus Christ. "For if we sin wilfully after that we have received the knowledge of the truth, there remaineth no more sacrifice for sins, but a certain fearful looking for of judgment and fiery indignation, which shall devour the adversaries" (Heb. 10:26–27).

Sins of ignorance reveal the underlying truth that man is a sinner by nature. My friend, I must say this to you: You are a sinner whether you know it or not. You are a sinner by nature, and so am I. That is the reason we commit sins. Regardless of the estimation of any given time or custom, man is a sinner. God's attitude toward sin does not change. We do those things which are contrary to God because it is impossible for the natural man to do anything that will please God. Natural man does not have that capacity. He is a sinner by nature. These sins must be called to man's attention. It is sin regardless of who commits it.

The sin offering gave a profound conviction of sin. This conviction stands out in the literature of the race. The deep guilt complex of man must be diagnosed before an adequate remedy can be prescribed.

Listen to the psalmist, "Search me, O God, and know my heart: try me, and know my thoughts: And see if there be any wicked way in me, and lead me in the way everlasting" (Ps. 139:23–24). "Against thee, thee only, have I sinned, and done this evil in thy sight: that thou mightest be justified when thou speakest, and be clear when thou judgest" (Ps. 51:4).

This is what I call getting on the Lord Jesus Christ's couch instead of going to the psychiatrist's couch. A great many people with a guilt complex go to the psychiatrists today. One would get the impression that the psychiatrist or psychologist has a skill that the Word of God does not reveal. I think that is a wrong impression. The Word of God contains the remedy for man today. If you have a problem and you are bothered with a guilt complex, a personality problem, why don't you go to the Lord's couch and cry out, "Search me, O God, and know my heart. Try me. See if there be any wicked way in me." My friend, our problem is not that our mothers didn't give us all the love we should have had when we were little brats; our problem is that we are sinners by nature. So let's get on God's couch and tell Him that.

The sins of ignorance were acts committed by a person who at the time did not know they were sin. "Who can understand his errors? cleanse thou me from secret faults" (Ps. 19:12). How we need to confess to God that we are sinful human beings! If you can't think of anything special to confess, then just confess who you are, a sinner.

A group of men gathered regularly for prayer and one man would always pray, "Lord, if we have committed any sin, forgive us." The men got tired of this little formula and one of them said to him, "Why don't you tell Him what the sin is?" The man answered, "Well, I don't know what it is." The leader said, "Why don't you take a guess at it?" And do you know, the man's first guess was right! We need to confess our sins to God!

If a man sinned through ignorance, rashness, or accident, God made provision for his deliverance. He established the cities of refuge (Num. 35:11). God has a refuge for you too, my friend; He has a remedy for you. "My little children, these things write I unto you, that ye sin not. And if any man sin, we have an advocate with the Father, Jesus Christ the righteous" (1 John 2:1).

Paul explains the reason he was the chief of sinners and why he obtained mercy. He was a blasphemer and a persecutor and injurious, but he obtained mercy because he did it ignorantly in unbelief. He goes on to say, "And the grace of our Lord was exceeding abundant with faith and love which is in Christ Jesus. This is a faithful saying, and worthy of all acceptation, that Christ Jesus came into the world to save sinners; of whom I am chief" (1 Tim. 1:14–15).

My dad died when I was fourteen, and soon I was obliged to go into the business world. There I teamed up with the wrong crowd. I was out doing things that a man twenty-five years old was doing, and I was just sixteen years old. I'm not offering an excuse, but I really didn't know then how bad it was. Then there came that day when I received Christ, and from that day to this, I look back and hate myself for what I did. Thank God, friend, there is a sin offering. Christ died for me; so I can go and tell Him all about it. I don't need to crawl up on anybody's couch and tell him about it. It's none of his business. But it sure is God's business and I must tell Him about it. He forgives me because He took care of all my sins at the Cross.

The sin offering teaches us that we must see ourselves as God sees us. It brings before us the consciousness of sin and our own unworthiness, but also God's provision. "I acknowledged my sin unto thee, and mine iniquity have I not hid. I said, I will confess my transgressions unto the LORD; and thou forgavest the iniquity of my sin" (Ps. 32:5). It lifts the guilt complex.

The sin offering taught its own inadequacy. "Sacrifice and offering thou didst not desire; mine ears hast thou opened: burnt offering and sin offering hast thou not required" (Ps. 40:6). It pointed the way to God's perfect satisfaction for sin and His forgiveness. "Having therefore, brethren, boldness to enter into the holiest by the blood of Jesus, by a new and living way, which he hath consecrated for us, through the veil, that is to say, his flesh; and having an high priest over the house of God; let us draw near with a true heart in full assurance of faith, having our hearts sprinkled from an evil conscience, and our bodies washed with pure water" (Heb. 10:19–22). Now you and I, sinners, can come into His presence with boldness. Why? Because Jesus is our sin offering, even for these sins of ignorance.

Sin through ignorance brings to our attention another side of God's justice and His absolute fairness in dealing with man. God will deal with man in equity. There will be degrees of punishment as there will be degrees of rewards. The degree of responsibility is also recognized in the sin offering as we shall see in the different classes of people who are considered here.

SINS OF THE PRIEST

If the priest that is anointed do sin according to the sin of the people; then let him bring for his sin, which he hath sinned, a young bullock without blemish unto the LORD for a sin offering [Lev. 4:3].

The sin of the priest is considered first, for he stood in the place of leadership. If he was wrong, the people were wrong. His sin was their sin. Like priest, like people. He was to bring a young bullock, the most valuable animal of all, as his offering. You see that the position of the one who sinned determined the type of animal for the sin sacrifice. His sin was no different, but his responsibility was greater.

It is still the same today. "Therefore to him that knoweth to do good, and doeth it not, to him it is sin" (James 4:17). "My brethren, be not many masters, knowing that we shall receive the greater condemnation" (James 3:1). Do you want to be a preacher? It makes you more responsible. Do you want to sing a solo? It makes you responsible. Do you want to be a deacon or an officer in the church, or a teacher of a Sunday school class? Then you are more responsible than anyone else. Privilege carries with it a responsibility, and God Himself will hold you to that responsibility.

That is what is clearly shown here. "According to the sins of the

people" could be more properly translated "so as to cause the people
to sin." This points out the responsibility of the priest. He was a mere
human being and he was subject to the same temptations as the remainder of the race. "For the law maketh men high priests which have
infirmity . . ." (Heb. 7:28). It is in this point that there is a radical
difference between Christ, our great High Priest, and the priests of the
order of Aaron. "For we have not an high priest which cannot be
touched with the feeling of our infirmities; but was in all points
tempted like as we are, yet without sin" (Heb. 4:15).

> **And he shall bring the bullock unto the door of the tab-
> ernacle of the congregation before the LORD; and shall
> lay his hand upon the bullock's head, and kill the bul-
> lock before the LORD [Lev. 4:4].**

This is the ritual for the sin offering. In this part of the ritual there is a
similarity to the burnt offering.

> **And the priest that is anointed shall take of the bullock's
> blood, and bring it to the tabernacle of the congregation:**
>
> **And the priest shall dip his finger in the blood, and
> sprinkle of the blood seven times before the LORD, before
> the veil of the sanctuary.**
>
> **And the priest shall put some of the blood upon the
> horns of the altar of sweet incense before the LORD,
> which is in the tabernacle of the congregation; and shall
> pour all the blood of the bullock at the bottom of the
> altar of the burnt offering, which is at the door of the
> tabernacle of the congregation [Lev. 4:5–7].**

To sprinkle the blood seven times before the veil secured God's relationship with the offender. To put some of the blood on the horns of
the altar of incense, the place of prayer, was to restore the privilege of
worship to the offender. Our acceptance by God and our worship of
Him are dependent upon the blood of Jesus Christ. "If we confess our

sins, he is faithful and just to forgive us our sins, and to cleanse us from all unrighteousness" (1 John 1:9). "And almost all things are by the law purged with blood; and without shedding of blood is no remission" (Heb. 9:22).

The remainder of the blood was poured out at the bottom of the brazen altar. This satisfied the conscience of the sinner and removed the guilt complex. This was the remedy for the conviction of sin and the only remedy that could satisfy the mind and heart.

My friend, the important thing for you to understand is that when Christ forgives you your sin, He also forgives you. There is nothing more to be said about it. He has put it in the bottom of the sea. He has removed it as far as the east is from the west. He has removed it so that He will not even remember it. He settles the sin question. That rids us of our guilt complexes. You need never wonder whether He has really forgiven you. He took away all your sin and guilt. *All* of it. When you come to Christ and see Him, you will find Him adequate.

And he shall take off from it all the fat of the bullock for the sin offering; the fat that covereth the inwards, and all the fat that is upon the inwards,

And the two kidneys, and the fat that is upon them, which is by the flanks, and the caul above the liver, with the kidneys, it shall he take away,

As it was taken off from the bullock of the sacrifice of peace offerings: and the priest shall burn them upon the altar of the burnt offering [Lev. 4:8–10].

Here the ritual of the sin sacrifice follows that of the peace offering. The sin has been forgiven. Fellowship is restored and service is again restored. The fat is offered to be burned on the altar. Remember that the fat represents the very best.

And the skin of the bullock, and all his flesh, with his head, and with his legs, and his inwards, and his dung,

Even the whole bullock shall he carry forth without the camp unto a clean place, where the ashes are poured out, and burn him on the wood with fire: where the ashes are poured out shall he be burnt [Lev. 4:11-12].

At this point there is a radical departure from the other offerings. The remainder of the bullock was taken without the camp and burned there. We believe that this is simply an emphasis upon the exceeding sinfulness of sin. This animal was the sin offering—there is no thought of consecration or signifying the person of Christ. Rather, this is Christ, the sin-bearer, the One who was made sin for us. This deeper meaning is given to us in Hebrews. "We have an altar, whereof they have no right to eat which serve the tabernacle. For the bodies of those beasts, whose blood is brought into the sanctuary by the high priest for sin, are burned without the camp. Wherefore Jesus also, that he might sanctify the people with his own blood, suffered without the gate. Let us go forth therefore unto him without the camp, bearing his reproach. For here have we no continuing city, but we seek one to come" (Heb. 13:10-14). Let us ponder this Scripture well. Religion can never satisfy the heart or meet the requirements of a God who is holy. Only the death of Christ on the Cross can give us forgiveness of sins. We are sinners by nature and we are not fit for heaven. If God would consign this entire world into a lost eternity, the angels in heaven would still sing, "Holy, holy, holy!" But thank God, He didn't do that. He loved us so much that He sent Jesus Christ to be made sin for us. Don't try to solve the problem of your sin in any other way than to turn and trust Christ. He is adequate. He meets the deep need in your heart and soul. He alone can offer you forgiveness for sin. The death of Christ on the Cross as our sin-bearer is the only solution there is to sin. That is the meaning of that part of the animal which had to be burned outside the camp.

SINS OF THE CONGREGATION

And if the whole congregation of Israel sin through ig-norance, and the thing be hid from the eyes of the as-sembly, and they have done somewhat against any of the

commandments of the LORD concerning things which should not be done, and are guilty;

When the sin, which they have sinned against it, is known, then the congregation shall offer a young bullock for the sin, and bring him before the tabernacle of the congregation [Lev. 4:13–14].

The victim for the entire congregation was the same as for the priest. A young bullock was the most valuable animal for offering. You see, the high priest represented the entire congregation before the Lord, so the requirement would be the same.

I think there is another lesson here. There is not only an individual responsibility before God but there is also a corporate responsibility. God judges nations, and many people who didn't participate in the sin of the nation are judged along with it.

When Jerusalem was destroyed in A.D. 70, the whole nation went into captivity. When the Roman Empire disintegrated, everyone went down with it. Friends, you and I are responsible since we are a part of the nation.

God also judges churches and local congregations. I hear people say that they are going to stay in a liberal church and try to witness to it. Where do they get that idea? It's not in the Word of God. If you identify yourself with a church which does not teach the truth from the Word of God, God will judge you right along with that church. Your responsibility is an individual responsibility, but when you join yourself with something, you are placed under corporate responsibility also. When the Lord sent His messages to the seven churches of Asia in the Book of Revelation, the message was to the churches and to every member of each church.

And the elders of the congregation shall lay their hands upon the head of the bullock before the LORD: and the bullock shall be killed before the LORD [Lev. 4:15].

The elders represented the nation. Similarly, the elders in the Book of Revelation represent the church.

Now the ritual here is identical with the offering of the priest. I'll not go over that again. It is explained in verses 16–21.

SINS OF THE RULER

When a ruler hath sinned, and done somewhat through ignorance against any of the commandments of the LORD his God concerning things which should not be done, and is guilty;

Or, if his sin, wherein he hath sinned, come to his knowledge; he shall bring his offering, a kid of the goats, a male without blemish [Lev. 4:22–23].

You will notice that all these different groups are to bring an offering because they are sinners. Their responsibility is different in each case, but they are all guilty. This has reference to a civil ruler. People who are rulers are often charged inaccurately and there is gossip about them. This must be real guilt. His sin must come to his knowledge and then he shall bring his offering. Again, the ruler is in a place of responsibility. His offering was of less worth than that of the priest or the entire congregation, but it was of more value than that of a private person.

This teaches us the lesson that rulers are ordained of God and thereby are responsible to God. Unfortunately, our politicians today do not seek to please God. I have listened to many of their speeches and I have yet to hear one of them, Democrat or Republican, say that he feels that he has a responsibility to God. They are always trying to please the people. You hear them talk of their constituents. God says that they are responsible to Him!

The ruler was to bring an offering of a kid of the goats, a male without blemish. The offering was not as valuable as the bullock. The ritual and the procedure for the offering for the ruler follow the same steps as that for the priest and for the people. You see, the sin of the man is the same as if he were a private citizen. The value of the animal he must sacrifice indicates the degree of his responsibility.

SINS OF THE COMMON PEOPLE

**And if any one of the common people sin through igno-
rance, while he doeth somewhat against any of the commandments of the LORD concerning things which ought
not to be done, and be guilty [Lev. 4:27].**

This is now talking about the common person, the private citizen.
The offering is for a sin through ignorance but a sin against a commandment of God. It is against something specifically stated as being
forbidden. His guilt cannot be just hearsay, but the guilt must be established.

Again, this offering was to lift the guilt complex and satisfy the
conscience. Only the death of Christ can lift the crushing guilt complex from modern man. Psychological procedures have not been able
to accomplish this. A person's conscience may be seared with a hot
iron and the guilt may be transferred from one area to another, but
deep in the human heart the strange guilt complex lingers. It is removed only when it is brought to Christ for His forgiveness.

**Or if his sin, which he hath sinned, come to his knowl-
edge: then he shall bring his offering, a kid of the goats,
a female without blemish, for his sin which he hath
sinned [Lev. 4:28].**

If a sin comes to his knowledge later, then it is no longer a sin through
ignorance, but it requires the same sacrifice. What does the believer
do today? He has come to Christ as a lost sinner and accepted Him as
his Savior. Then, when he finds that he has sinned, he confesses it to
God. "If we confess our sins, he is faithful and just to forgive us our
sins, and to cleanse us from all unrighteousness" (1 John 1:9).

A female kid of the goats was an offering of less value than any
previous offering. Yet, an offering was required. All of these offerings
point to the death of Christ.

Again, the ritual is the same for all classifications of humanity. A female lamb was also acceptable according to verse 32, and again the ritual of the lamb was the same.

The important clause to notice is, "it shall be forgiven him" in verse 31 and verse 35. The important truth is that complete forgiveness was secured for the sinner. Total absolution was accomplished. This is exactly what was accomplished for us when Christ died. "In whom we have redemption through his blood, the forgiveness of sins, according to the riches of his grace" (Eph. 1:7).

THE LAW OF THE SIN OFFERING

And the Lord spake unto Moses, saying,

Speak unto Aaron and to his sons, saying, This is the law of the sin offering: In the place where the burnt offering is killed shall the sin offering be killed before the Lord: it is most holy [Lev. 6:24–25].

The place for the sin offering was the same as the place for the burnt offering. Both refer to Christ.

The priest that offereth it for sin shall eat it: in the holy place shall it be eaten, in the court of the tabernacle of the congregation.

Whatsoever shall touch the flesh thereof shall be holy: and when there is sprinkled of the blood thereof upon any garment, thou shalt wash that whereon it was sprinkled in the holy place [Lev. 6:26–27].

The sin offering was holy. You remember that Christ on the Cross cried out to God with words from Psalm 22. "My God, my God, why hast thou forsaken me? why art thou so far from helping me, and from the words of my roaring? O my God, I cry in the daytime, but thou hearest not; and in the night season, and am not silent. But thou art holy, O thou that inhabitest the praises of Israel" (Ps. 22:1–3).

Christ became sin for us on the Cross and yet He was holy. God withdrew from Him and yet God was in Christ reconciling the world to Himself. I don't understand it; this is a great mystery. He was holy and is still holy yet our sin was put on Him. We will never know or understand what He suffered on the Cross; because He is holy and since we are not, we do not know what suffering really is.

> **But the earthen vessel wherein it is sodden shall be broken: and if it be sodden in a brasen pot, it shall be both scoured, and rinsed in water.**
>
> **All the males among the priests shall eat thereof: it is most holy.**
>
> **And no sin offering, whereof any of the blood is brought into the tabernacle of the congregation to reconcile withal in the holy place, shall be eaten: it shall be burnt in the fire [Lev. 6:28–30].**

The law is meticulous even concerning the vessels. You see, the offering was for sin, and sin is the opposite of holiness. God is giving the final reminder of this.

"Let the wicked forsake his way, and the unrighteous man his thoughts: and let him return unto the LORD, and he will have mercy upon him; and to our God, for he will abundantly pardon. For my thoughts are not your thoughts, neither are your ways my ways, saith the LORD. For as the heavens are higher than the earth, so are my ways higher than your ways, and my thoughts than your thoughts" (Isa. 55:7–9). We need to be reminded of the fact that He saved us *from* sin, not *to* sin. That is very important for us to note. Paul writes, "What shall we say then? Shall we continue in sin, that grace may abound? God forbid. How shall we, that are dead to sin, live any longer therein?" (Rom. 6:1–2).

CHAPTER 5

THEME: The trespass offering: specific acts of sin committed in ignorance; non-specific acts of sin committed in ignorance

Some expositors treat the first 13 verses of this chapter as part of the sin offering. There is ample justification for this, as the word *trespass* in verses 6 and 7 can be translated "guilt" and should be "for his guilt." In verses 6, 7, 9, and 11, the sin offering is required for the trespass because the act of sin is caused by the nature of sin. All sin comes from the same source: the sin nature. You and I inherited it from Adam. The ax must be laid at the root as well as at the fruit.

In our discussion here, we shall treat the entire chapter as the trespass offering. The word *trespass* has very much the same meaning in the King James translation as it does in present-day use of the word. We all understand a "No Trespassing" sign. It means we are not to invade the rights of others. Liberty is a word which is much misused and abused today. Many folk go around parading, burning things, destroying things, and talking about liberty. Friend, you are free to swing your fist in any direction that you please, but your liberty ends where my nose begins. A trespass is the invasion of the rights of either God or man.

For example, withholding tithes from God was counted a trespass in Israel. We have the example of Achan who took the accursed thing and this was considered a trespass (Josh. 7:1).

We must always remember that our trespasses arise out of our sin nature. Man is totally depraved and actually has no capacity for God whatsoever. God makes it very clear that He cannot and will not accept the works of unsaved men to accomplish their salvation. Their righteousness is as filthy rags. He does not save by works of righteousness, but He saves us by His grace. It is impossible for an unsaved man to please God "Because the carnal mind is enmity against God: for it is not subject to the law of God, neither indeed can be" (Rom. 8:7). When Jesus was on this earth, religious folk came to Him with this question, "Then said they unto him, What shall we do, that we might work the works of God? Jesus answered and said unto them, This is the work of God, that ye believe on him whom he hath sent" (John 6:28–29). The apostles had the same answer, " . . . Believe on the Lord Jesus Christ, and thou shalt be saved . . . " (Acts 16:31).

SPECIFIC ACTS OF SIN COMMITTED IN IGNORANCE

The list of sins enumerated here is obviously not an exhaustive list but gives us examples of a limitless number which could be named. These are sins of individuals, not of the entire congregation. Most of the section deals with the remedy and not the disease. So we find the emphasis is upon the type of offering and not on the character of the offerer, as it was in the sin offering.

> **And if a soul sin, and hear the voice of swearing, and is a witness, whether he hath seen or known of it; if he do not utter it, then he shall bear his iniquity [Lev. 5:1].**

Let me say again that the four specific sins listed here are merely examples. I think one could fill up the rest of the Book of Leviticus with specific sins if one named them all. I understand some preacher made up a list of 800 specific sins that he had thought of. He was swamped with letters from people who wanted the list of sins. They thought maybe there was something they were missing since they couldn't think of 800 sins. Well, here we are given a few examples.

"And if a soul sin, and hear the voice of swearing" could be better translated, "if a person sin in this respect that he hears the voice of adjuration." It has to do with the hearing of an oath and being a witness. If a witness has seen or knows something, but he withholds the truth to the detriment of some individual, then that is a sin of omission.

There are sins of omission today. Some folk come into church today thinking their hands are clean because they haven't murdered or stolen. Listen to James: "Therefore to him that knoweth to do good, and doeth it not, to him it is sin" (James 4:17).

Solomon prayed to God concerning this very issue of not telling the truth when a witness ought to tell the truth. "If any man trespass against his neighbour, and an oath be laid upon him to cause him to swear, and the oath come before thine altar in this house: then hear thou in heaven, and do, and judge thy servants, condemning the wicked, to bring his way upon his head; and justifying the righteous, to give him according to his righteousness" (1 Kings 8:31–32).

Let me give you an example of this. The town gossip is crossing the square of the town and she sees the president of the bank crossing the street. His secretary is also leaving the bank to go to lunch and a car hits her as she is crossing the street. The bank president rushes over and picks her up in his arms and takes her into a doctor's office. The gossip runs to the telephone to call the wife of the bank president and says, "Do you know, Madge, I saw your husband with another woman in his arms!" Now although that was a fact, it wasn't the whole truth! She is withholding important information. This is a sin of omission.

I was in a meeting of Christian men who were talking about the pastor and they gave certain information that was accurate. But it wasn't the whole truth. They told only a part of it; they didn't tell the whole situation. They were willing to let that group of men believe that they had heard the whole story. That is a trespass. It is one of the most vicious sins that can be committed. Notice here that it is Number One on God's Sin Parade! Over in the Book of Proverbs we find a list of things which God hates and in that list of seven we find "a lying tongue" (Prov. 6:17).

You remember that Jesus was quiet during most of His trial. We are told that He held His peace. But when He was put under oath, He broke His silence. Then He was no longer dumb like a sheep before her shearers is dumb. ". . . And the high priest answered and said unto him, I adjure thee by the living God, that thou tell us whether thou be the Christ, the Son of God. Jesus saith unto him, Thou hast said: nevertheless I say unto you, hereafter shall ye see the Son of man sitting

on the right hand of power, and coming in the clouds of heaven"
(Matt. 26:63–64). You see, under oath He did not hold His peace, but
spoke out in witness. He told the whole truth.

> **Or if a soul touch any unclean thing, whether it be a
> carcase of an unclean beast, or a carcase of unclean cat-
> tle, or the carcase of unclean creeping things, and if it
> be hidden from him; he also shall be unclean, and
> guilty [Lev. 5:2].**

This is the law concerning uncleanness. A man might become polluted by contact with a dead animal without being aware of it while
others witnessed it. A dead carcase caused uncleanness by contact.
Why? Probably for health reasons.

This also speaks to Christians today. We can't be out in the world
without becoming unclean by seeing things and hearing things and
thinking things. We are unclean. We may not even realize that we
have come into contact with the unclean. It may be hidden from us so
we are not even aware of it. But we are not to rush into God's presence
until we are cleansed. This is why the psalmist says, "Who can understand his errors? cleanse thou me from secret faults" (Ps. 19:12).

We should not only pray for forgiveness in general, we are to name
our specific failures to God and ask Him for forgiveness. But more
than that, we should pray for forgiveness of sins that we may be un-
aware of. Sometimes we are unclean and do not realize it.

> **Or if he touch the uncleanness of man, whatsoever un-
> cleanness it be that a man shall be defiled withal, and it
> be hid from him; when he knoweth of it, then he shall be
> guilty [Lev. 5:3].**

This is similar to the case of the unclean animal, yet God makes a
distinction between man and beast. The penalty for this is more severe than for touching the beast (Lev. 11:24 and Num. 19:11–16). Apparently there were other distinctions of uncleanness concerning man
other than death.

> Or if a soul swear, pronouncing with his lips to do evil,
> or to do good, whatsoever it be that a man shall pro-
> nounce with an oath, and it be hid from him; when he
> knoweth of it, then he shall be guilty in one of these [Lev.
> 5:4].

Careless speech is involved in this instance. Sometimes we promise to do something, and then we don't do it. We promise that we will serve the Lord. Jephthah is an example of a man promising to do something very rash—to offer his daughter. Simon Peter boldly declared that he would not deny Christ, but would die defending Him.

Today I hear people making some very rash promises. In fact, I think some of our songs are dynamite, to tell the truth. In our songs we promise to give all to Him, to follow Him, to die for Him. We sing them so glibly that we don't even know what we are singing.

Also I think it is careless speech and presumptuous when we try to demand of God an answer to our prayers. We need always to remember that our prayers are to be in accordance with His will. If we ask anything according to His will, He hears us. Where did we get the idea that we could demand anything of God?

"Then he shall be guilty in one of these" refers to the four things which have been listed. Many more could have been included.

> And it shall be, when he shall be guilty in one of these
> things, that he shall confess that he hath sinned in that
> thing:
>
> And he shall bring his trespass offering unto the LORD
> for his sin which he hath sinned, a female from the
> flock, a lamb or a kid of the goats, for a sin offering: and
> the priest shall make an atonement for him concerning
> his sin [Lev. 5:5–6].

Confession is commanded for the first time. The other offerings were an open admission of guilt. This one has to do with secret sins. They were hidden sins even though they were against God and man.

You remember in Joshua 7, when Achan took the wedge of gold and the Babylonish garment, that trespass had to be dealt with publicly because it was that kind of sin. The laying on of hands in the other offerings was evidently an admission of sin. Here confession must come first, then the offering. In the sweet savor offerings, the offerings preceded any thought of confession. The opposite is true here.

I think this is what our Lord had in mind in the Sermon on the Mount. "Therefore if thou bring thy gift to the altar, and there rememberest that thy brother hath aught against thee; leave there thy gift before the altar, and go thy way; first be reconciled to thy brother, and then come and offer thy gift" (Matt. 5:23–24). The believer today is to confess his sin to God privately but he is to make restitution to the injured party.

The trespass offering simply means the offering of guilt. It was a sin offering, since all sin stems from the sin nature. We are not sinners because we sin; we sin because we are sinners with a sin nature.

Since this offering is for an act of sin which is one of the many facets of the sin nature, the value of the offering was not as great as the value of the sin offering in chapter 4.

And if he be not able to bring a lamb, then he shall bring for his trespass, which he hath committed, two turtledoves, or two young pigeons, unto the LORD; one for a sin offering, and the other for a burnt offering [Lev. 5:7].

The emphasis in the trespass offering is not in the character or position of the offerer, but in the sacrifice itself. Two turtledoves were required, as one was for a sin offering and one was for a burnt offering. The person and the work of Christ are represented in the poorest of offerings. This was the sacrifice of the poor. Christ preached glad tidings to the poor.

Notice that it is labeled a sin offering because it arises from the sin nature.

> And he shall bring them unto the priest, who shall offer
> that which is for the sin offering first, and wring off his
> head from his neck, but shall not divide it asunder:

> And he shall sprinkle of the blood of the sin offering
> upon the side of the altar; and the rest of the blood shall
> be wrung out at the bottom of the altar: it is a sin offer-
> ing [Lev. 5:8–9].

Blood must be shed, though the head of the bird was not removed
from the body.

> And he shall offer the second for a burnt offering, ac-
> cording to the manner: and the priest shall make an
> atonement for him for his sin which he hath sinned, and
> it shall be forgiven him [Lev. 5:10].

The sinner has complete forgiveness even with the little bird. All of
this points to Christ as the one sacrifice.

> But if he be not able to bring two turtledoves, or two
> young pigeons, then he that sinned shall bring for his
> offering the tenth part of an ephah of fine flour for a sin
> offering; he shall put no oil upon it, neither shall he put
> any frankincense thereon: for it is a sin offering [Lev.
> 5:11].

The poorest of the poor was not left out. If one could not bring a bird,
he could bring what amounted to a piece of bread. This sacrifice was
still a substitute for him.

> Then shall he bring it to the priest, and the priest shall
> take his handful of it, even a memorial thereof, and burn
> it on the altar, according to the offerings made by fire
> unto the Lord: it is a sin offering.

And the priest shall make an atonement for him as touching his sin that he hath sinned in one of these, and it shall be forgiven him: and the remnant shall be the priest's, as a meat offering [Lev. 5:12-13].

NON-SPECIFIC ACTS OF SIN COMMITTED IN IGNORANCE

And the LORD spake unto Moses, saying,

If a soul commit a trespass, and sin through ignorance, in the holy things of the LORD; then he shall bring for his trespass unto the LORD a ram without blemish out of the flocks, with thy estimation by shekels of silver, after the shekel of the sanctuary, for a trespass offering.

And he shall make amends for the harm that he hath done in the holy thing, and shall add the fifth part thereto, and give it unto the priest: and the priest shall make an atonement for him with the ram of the trespass offering, and it shall be forgiven him [Lev. 5:14-16].

These trespass offerings emphasize the fact that there has been an invasion of the rights of both God and man. Harm to others is the feature which requires that reparation had to be performed. The principal had to be restored *plus* a fifth part. This must be what Zacchaeus had in mind when he told the Lord that he would give half his goods to the poor and restore fourfold what he had taken from any man by false accusation (Luke 19:8).

The chief wrong committed through ignorance seems to apply to robbing God in connection with tithes and offerings. We find this again in Malachi: "Will a man rob God? Yet ye have robbed me. But ye say, Wherein have we robbed thee? In tithes and offerings. Ye are cursed with a curse: for ye have robbed me, even this whole nation" (Mal. 3:8-9). The Lord promises them blessing if they will bring their tithes, such blessing that there shall not be room to receive it.

Ecclesiastes 5:5 warns, "Better is it that thou shouldest not vow, than that thou shouldest vow and not pay." For this kind of neglect, this trespass against God, the offering must be valuable. It must be a ram. This points us to Christ, who is precious. "But with the precious blood of Christ, as of a lamb without blemish and without spot" (1 Pet. 1:19). Through this offering there was forgiveness for the sinner who committed the trespass in ignorance.

> **And if a soul sin, and commit any of these things which are forbidden to be done by the commandments of the LORD; though he wist it not, yet is he guilty, and shall bear his iniquity.**
>
> **And he shall bring a ram without blemish out of the flock, with thy estimation, for a trespass offering, unto the priest: and the priest shall make an atonement for him concerning his ignorance wherein he erred and wist it not, and it shall be forgiven him.**
>
> **It is a trespass offering: he hath certainly trespassed against the LORD [Lev. 5:17–19].**

This apparently had to do with breaking any of the commandments of God in ignorance. Ignorance of the law is no excuse. This is also true in civil law. In spite of the lack of knowledge of the commandment, the offender was guilty and was held liable. Here again, the ram is given as the only animal for the trespass offering.

This offering in its ritual followed the pattern of the sin offering, except in the sprinkling of the blood, which followed the pattern of the burnt and peace offerings. We will see this in more detail in chapter 7.

CHAPTER 6

THEME: Conclusion of rules concerning the trespass offering; law concerning the burnt offering; concerning the meal offering; concerning the sin offering

Chapters 6 and 7 present the law of the offerings. Actually, the law of the offerings concerned the priests and their particular part in them and portion of them. It could be called the special rules for the priests who minister at the altar of God.

This section opens with specific directions to the priests and a command for Aaron and his sons. Since the priests served at the altar, they were involved in all of the offerings that were made on the burnt altar. All of this is a shadow of the reality in heaven where Christ, our great High Priest, serves. "For every high priest is ordained to offer gifts and sacrifices: wherefore it is of necessity that this man have somewhat also to offer. For if he were on earth, he should not be a priest, seeing that there are priests that offer gifts according to the law: who serve unto the example and shadow of heavenly things, as Moses was admonished of God when he was about to make the tabernacle: for, See, saith he, that thou make all things according to the pattern shewed to thee in the mount" (Heb. 8:3–5).

There is another striking feature. Christ is not only the priest but He is also the sacrifice. He offered Himself. "Wherefore when he cometh into the world, he saith, Sacrifice and offering thou wouldest not, but a body hast thou prepared me: in burnt offerings and sacrifices for sin thou hast had no pleasure. Then said I, Lo, I come (in the volume of the book it is written of me,) to do thy will, O God. Above when he said, Sacrifice and offering and burnt offerings and offering for sin thou wouldest not, neither hadst pleasure therein; which are offered by the law; then said he, Lo, I come to do thy will, O God. He taketh away the first, that he may establish the second. By the which will we are sanctified through the offering of the body of Jesus Christ once for all. And every priest standeth daily ministering and offering often times the same sacrifices, which can never take away sins: But this man, after he had offered one sacrifice for sins for ever, sat down on the right hand of God" (Heb. 10:5–12).

We need to be so aware of this today. There are a great many religions which have elaborate rituals with marching and robes and candles and routines. I suppose in all our churches we do a lot of things that really are not worthwhile. God is a Spirit and must be worshiped in spirit and in truth. God gave us this great spiritual truth here in the book of Hebrews so that we would see that.

You and I have a High Priest in heaven and He is just as busy as can be. When it says that He sat down, it means that redemption was complete. It is similar to saying that God rested on the seventh day because creation was complete. It doesn't mean that He was tired and stopped doing anything. Just so, the Lord Jesus doesn't sit down because He is tired and doesn't want to do anything. He is busy! He died down here on this earth to save us. He lives up at the right hand of God to keep us saved. You and I ought to keep in touch with Him. This is reality! This is spiritual! The trouble today is that we are out of touch with the *living* Christ. He is no longer a reality to us.

The greatest compliment I ever heard given about a preacher was for the one whom I succeeded in Nashville, Tennessee. A butcher in the market said to me, "I understand you are following Dr. Allen. You know, there is something about that man. Every time I meet him, I feel like he just left Jesus around the corner." I want to tell you, friends, Dr. Allen meant business with Jesus. Jesus Christ was a reality in his life.

CONCLUSION OF RULES CONCERNING
THE TRESPASS OFFERING

Again, the sins listed are merely examples of a longer list of trespasses which could be given. They are sins committed against one's neighbor in the daily run of affairs.

And the LORD spake unto Moses, saying,

If a soul sin, and commit a trespass against the LORD, and lie unto his neighbour in that which was delivered

him to keep, or in fellowship, or in a thing taken away by violence, or hath deceived his neighbour;

Or have found that which was lost, and lieth concerning it, and sweareth falsely; in any of all these that a man doeth, sinning therein:

Then it shall be, because he hath sinned, and is guilty, that he shall restore that which he took violently away, or the thing which he hath deceitfully gotten, or that which was delivered him to keep, or the lost thing which he found.

Or all that about which he hath sworn falsely; he shall even restore it in the principal, and shall add the fifth part more thereto, and give it unto him to whom it appertaineth, in the day of his trespass offering.

And he shall bring his trespass offering unto the LORD, a ram without blemish out of the flock, with thy estimation, for a trespass offering, unto the priest:

And the priest shall make an atonement for him before the LORD: and it shall be forgiven him for any thing of all that he hath done in trespassing therein [Lev. 6:1–7].

This would appear to be a separate revelation from God, distinct from the preceding chapter. It shows that sin against a neighbor is a sin against God. That is why Jesus said, "Therefore all things whatsoever ye would that men should do to you, do ye even so to them: for this is the law and the prophets" (Matt. 7:12).

Certain specific sins are mentioned here. Lying about borrowed articles and responsibility for articles left for safe keeping are mentioned. We find an example of this in 2 Kings 6:5 when the students of Elisha lost the borrowed ax. "Fellowship" in this passage actually refers to a business partnership. "Taking by violence" would be a forced transaction such as Ahab taking Naboth's vineyard in 1 Kings 21:2–16. "Deceiving his neighbor" would mean lying to the neighbor in not reporting having found a lost article.

May I say again, sins against one's fellowman are also sins against God. We see here again that restitution had to be made with an additional penalty of one-fifth added. A fifth would be a double tithe. This was followed by the trespass offering. Again, it is the ram that is the victim. God is showing that He is no respecter of persons.

The trespass offering was vital to the spiritual life of the individual Israelite. "Fools make a mock at sin: but among the righteous there is favour" (Prov. 14:9). A sense of sin renders Jesus precious to the soul.

LAW CONCERNING THE BURNT OFFERING

And the Lord spake unto Moses, saying,

Command Aaron and his sons, saying, This is the law of the burnt offering: It is the burnt offering because of the burning upon the altar all night unto the morning and the fire of the altar shall be burning in it [Lev. 6:8–9].

The fire on the altar was to burn continually, that is, while the tabernacle was set up and not on the wilderness march. The burnt offering was left on the altar all night and the fire was kept burning so that the whole offering would be consumed.

This speaks of the continual consecration of Christ. It was the Lord Jesus who could say, " . . . I do always those things that please him" (John 8:29). He displays this love and obedience in His high priestly prayer, "And for their sakes I sanctify myself, that they also might be sanctified through the truth" (John 17:19). Or listen to Him in John 4:31–32: "In the meanwhile his disciples prayed him, saying, Master, eat. But he said unto them, I have meat to eat that ye know not of."

This also speaks of the fact that we are to offer ourselves a living sacrifice to God (Rom. 12:1–2). I find that when I crawl upon the altar and the fire gets hot, I crawl off. I don't know about you, but I see a lot of folk doing that too. I wish I could say that I always do the things that please Him. The Lord Jesus could say it, but I can't. There is a challenge to every believer today because God delights in the continual obedience of His children. That should give us real food for thought.

Remember that this was the issue when Samuel rebuked King Saul. "And Samuel said, Hath the LORD as great delight in burnt offerings and sacrifices, as in obeying the voice of the LORD? Behold, to obey is better than sacrifice, and to hearken than the fat of rams. For rebellion is as the sin of witchcraft, and stubbornness is as iniquity and idolatry. Because thou hast rejected the word of the LORD, he hath also rejected thee from being king" (1 Sam. 15:22–23).

Today you and I need to offer our own hearts and lives to Him, if we belong to Him, that is, if we are saved. God forbid that we simply make empty professions. What is it that God wants us to do? " . . . This is the work of God, that ye believe on him whom he hath sent" (John 6:29).

And the priest shall put on his linen garment, and his linen breeches shall he put upon his flesh, and take up the ashes which the fire hath consumed with the burnt offering on the altar, and he shall put them beside the altar.

And he shall put off his garments, and put on other garments, and carry forth the ashes without the camp unto a clean place [Lev. 6:10–11].

God gave instructions even to the detail of the garment the priest was to wear. He was not only to put on the long robe, which was common to all the priests, but also the linen breeches. Why? The flesh must be covered totally. God is teaching that He *cannot* accept the works of the flesh.

"Now the works of the flesh are manifest, which are these; adultery, fornication, uncleanness, lasciviousness, idolatry, witchcraft, hatred, variance, emulations, wrath, strife, seditions, heresies, envyings, murders, drunkenness, revellings, and such like: of the which I tell you before, as I have also told you in time past, that they which do such things shall not inherit the kingdom of God" (Gal. 5:19–21). God cannot accept the works of the flesh. It is only the fruit of the Holy Spirit which is acceptable to Him. The Spirit of God must produce this in our lives. "But the fruit of the Spirit is love, joy, peace, longsuffering, gentleness, goodness, faith, meekness, temperance: against such there is no law" (Gal. 5:22–23).

The priest removed the garments he wore when he removed the ashes, and he put on a fresh suit. This was a continual reminder of the utter pollution of sin. The ashes of the altar spoke primarily of the judgment of sin, and even the ashes were contaminated. They must be taken out and put in a clean place. What a picture this is of the defilement of sin!

> And the fire upon the altar shall be burning in it; it shall not be put out: and the priest shall burn wood on it every morning, and lay the burnt offering in order upon it; and he shall burn thereon the fat of the peace offerings.
>
> The fire shall ever be burning upon the altar; it shall never go out [Lev. 6:12–13].

This is another reminder that the fire is to burn continually and is repeated again in verse 13. A fresh supply of wood was to be made in the morning and a burnt offering made for the whole camp. This was the morning sacrifice. The peace offering was then put on the burnt offering.

The continual burning on the altar should remind us that the fire of God burns continually. For those who reject Jesus Christ, this means the fire of God's wrath. "He that believeth on the Son hath everlasting life: and he that believeth not the Son shall not see life; but the wrath of God abideth on him" (John 3:36).

CONCERNING THE MEAL OFFERING

> And this is the law of the meat offering: the sons of Aaron shall offer it before the LORD, before the altar.
>
> And he shall take of it his handful, of the flour of the meat offering, and of the oil thereof, and all the frankincense which is upon the meat offering, and shall burn it

> upon the altar for a sweet savour, even the memorial of
> it, unto the LORD [Lev. 6:14–15].

Again the instructions are directed to the priests. The offerer is a worshiper who stands before the altar rejoicing before God. The priest performs for him.

> And the remainder thereof shall Aaron and his sons eat:
> with unleavened bread shall it be eaten in the holy
> place; in the court of the tabernacle of the congregation
> they shall eat it.
>
> It shall not be baken with leaven. I have given it unto
> them for their portion of my offerings made by fire; it is
> most holy, as is the sin offering, and as the trespass of-
> fering [Lev. 6:16–17].

"With unleavened bread shall it be eaten" is translated in the Septuagint, "unleavened shall it be eaten." The holy place where it was eaten was evidently the outer court of the tabernacle. It was holy because God was there. God's presence makes any place holy. Remember Moses was told to take off his shoes because the ground on which he stood was *holy* ground (Exod. 3:5). And Peter says that at the Transfiguration, they were with Him in the *holy* mount (2 Pet. 1:18).

> All the males among the children of Aaron shall eat of
> it. It shall be a statute for ever in your generations con-
> cerning the offerings of the LORD made by fire: every one
> that toucheth them shall be holy [Lev. 6:18].

All believers can participate in the enjoyment of the beauties and glories of the holy humanity of our Lord. My friend, you and I need to rejoice in Him more than we do.

> And the LORD spake unto Moses, saying,
>
> This is the offering of Aaron and of his sons, which they
> shall offer unto the LORD in the day when he is anointed;

the tenth part of an ephah of fine flour for a meat offering perpetual, half of it in the morning, and half thereof at night.

In a pan it shall be made with oil; and when it is baken, thou shalt bring it in: and the baken pieces of the meat offering shalt thou offer for a sweet savour unto the LORD.

And the priest of his sons that is anointed in his stead shall offer it: it is a statute for ever unto the LORD; it shall be wholly burnt.

For every meat offering for the priest shall be wholly burnt: it shall not be eaten [Lev. 6:19–23].

The priests were not only to eat but also they were to offer a tithe of the meal offering. The priest who received a tenth was in turn to offer a tenth. All of the tithe must be offered. The priests must give as well as receive.

Ministers today should set an example for their congregations in the matter of giving. The offering plate should be passed to the members of the church staff even if they are sitting on the platform during a service. We are all to have a part in giving.

CONCERNING THE SIN OFFERING

And the LORD spake unto Moses, saying,

Speak unto Aaron and to his sons, saying, This is the law of the sin offering: In the place where the burnt offering is killed shall the sin offering be killed before the LORD; it is most holy.

The priest that offereth it for sin shall eat it: in the holy place shall it be eaten, in the court of the tabernacle of the congregation.

Whatsoever shall touch the flesh thereof shall be holy: and when there is sprinkled of the blood thereof upon any garment, thou shalt wash that whereon it was sprinkled in the holy place.

But the earthen vessel wherein it is sodden shall be broken: and if it be sodden in a brasen pot, it shall be both scoured, and rinsed in water.

All the males among the priests shall eat thereof: it is most holy.

And no sin offering, whereof any of the blood is brought into the tabernacle of the congregation to reconcile withal in the holy place, shall be eaten: it shall be burnt in the fire [Lev. 6:24–30].

The instructions are again given to the priests. The sin offering, which speaks of the work of Christ on the Cross, was to be offered where the burnt offering was sacrificed. The burnt offering speaks of the person of Christ. Christ must be holy, harmless, and free from sin to be a satisfactory offering for sin. He must be able to save. This is why the virgin birth is essential in the plan of salvation. This is the One who was conceived by the Holy Spirit in a virgin. The sin offering was holy because Christ was free from sin—though He was made sin for us. It was my sin and your sin that caused Him to die, not His sin. He didn't die simply because He was arrested by the Romans. He could have stepped off this earth at any moment. He told Peter that He could call for legions of angels, if He wished to do so. He was made sin for us and He died in our place.

CHAPTER 7

THEME: *Concerning the trespass offering; concerning the peace offering*

The instructions to the priests are continued for these two offerings. These two offerings were more personal than the others. The trespass concerned the individual Israelite, and was not a congregational matter. The peace must finally be enjoyed by the individual in the body of believers.

The emphasis is upon the service of the priest. This is a picture of what the Lord Jesus has done and is doing for us today at God's right hand. He is still girded with the towel of service. He still cleanses. "If we confess our sins, he is faithful and just to forgive us our sins, and to cleanse us from all unrighteousness" (1 John 1:9).

CONCERNING THE TRESPASS OFFERING

Likewise this is the law of the trespass offering: it is most holy.

In the place where they kill the burnt offering shall they kill the trespass offering: and the blood thereof shall he sprinkle round about upon the altar.

And he shall offer of it all the fat thereof; the rump, and the fat that covereth the inwards,

And the two kidneys, and the fat that is on them, which is by the flanks, and the caul that is above the liver, with the kidneys, it shall he take away:

And the priest shall burn them upon the altar for an offering made by fire unto the Lord: it is a trespass offering.

Every male among the priests shall eat thereof: it shall be eaten in the holy place: it is most holy.

As the sin offering is, so is the trespass offering: there is one law for them: the priest that maketh atonement therewith shall have it [Lev. 7:1–7].

The ritual of the trespass offering follows the same pattern as that of the sin offering. Although it is for acts of sin, the offerer is reminded that the sacrifice is holy. The worth and merit of Christ cannot be over-emphasized. When we see our sin nature and our sinful acts in all their enormity and frightfulness, then we shall see the wonder, greatness, and holiness of Christ. My friend, you will never appreciate the Lord Jesus as your Savior until you see yourself as the terrible sinner that you are. I'm not calling you a low-down sinner. That is what the *Word of God* calls each one of us.

The blood is mentioned but is not emphasized as it is in the sin offering. We are told, however, that there is one law for them. There is a danger that we may tend to make the blood a commonplace thing. It should be dealt with reverently and reticently. It is precious, and we should be on guard that we do not treat that which is precious and holy as if it were commonplace.

And the priest that offereth any man's burnt offering, even the priest shall have to himself the skin of the burnt offering which he hath offered [Lev. 7:8].

Actually there was one part of the animal that was not burned. It was the skin, and that went to the priest. This speaks of being covered or clothed in the righteousness of Christ. God is satisfied with the Lord Jesus, and He sees us as being in Christ. "Even the righteousness of God which is by faith of Jesus Christ unto all and upon all them that believe: for there is no difference" (Rom. 3:22). Being clothed in Christ's righteousness is what Jesus referred to in His parable of the wedding feast. The man who entered without being clothed in a wedding garment was bound and cast out (Matt. 22:11–13).

> And all the meat offering that is baken in the oven, and
> all that is dressed in the fryingpan, and in the pan,
> shall be the priest's that offereth it.

> And every meat offering, mingled with oil, and dry,
> shall all the sons of Aaron have, one as much as another
> [Lev. 7:9–10].

Everything baked in the oven or dressed in the frying pan was to be for
the priests. This particular type of meal offering went to the priests in
its entirety.

CONCERNING THE PEACE OFFERING

> And this is the law of the sacrifice of peace offerings,
> which he shall offer unto the LORD.

> If he offer it for a thanksgiving, then he shall offer with
> the sacrifice of thanksgiving unleavened cakes mingled
> with oil, and unleavened wafers anointed with oil, and
> cakes mingled with oil, of fine flour, fried [Lev.
> 7:11–12].

The emphasis here is upon the fact that it must be a freewill offering.
The reason is for thanksgiving. This has a special meaning for believers. "By him therefore let us offer the sacrifice of praise to God continually, that is, the fruit of our lips giving thanks to his name" (Heb.
13:15). The fruit of our lips should be giving thanks to His name.
Friend, we cannot come to church to worship unless we are prepared
to offer the sacrifice of praise to God. A complaining, criticizing
Christian is in no position to worship God. How important this is!

> Besides the cakes, he shall offer for his offering leavened
> bread with the sacrifice of thanksgiving of his peace of-
> ferings.

> And of it he shall offer one out of the whole oblation for
> an heave offering unto the LORD, and it shall be the

**priest's that sprinkleth the blood of the peace offerings
[Lev. 7:13–14].**

Notice this very carefully. In verse 12, the cakes and wafers were to be unleavened. In verse 13, the bread was to be leavened. This seems strange. Why should this be when leaven is a principle of evil? It is because in verse 12 it is showing Christ as our peace offering and he is without sin, without leaven. In verse 13, it is the offerer who gives thanks for his participation in the peace. His sins have been forgiven and he has peace with God but there is still evil in him; leaven is still present. Peace with God does not depend on the believer attaining sinless perfection. The leaven is still there. Oh, how important it is to realize this! "If we say that we have no sin, we deceive ourselves, and the truth is not in us" (1 John 1:8). The believer is to confess his sin for forgiveness and cleansing, then he is to walk by the new nature in the power of the Holy Spirit. "For sin shall not have dominion over you . . ." (Rom. 6:14). The leavened bread was a heave offering. It was to be elevated toward heaven. Just so, our hearts are to be opened to God for Him to search us and know us and to lead us in the way everlasting (Ps. 139:23–24).

And the flesh of the sacrifice of his peace offerings for thanksgiving shall be eaten the same day that it is offered; he shall not leave any of it until the morning.

But if the sacrifice of his offering be a vow, or a voluntary offering, it shall be eaten the same day that he offereth his sacrifice: and on the morrow also the remainder of it shall be eaten:

But the remainder of the flesh of the sacrifice on the third day shall be burnt with fire.

And if any of the flesh of the sacrifice of his peace offerings be eaten at all on the third day, it shall not be accepted, neither shall it be imputed unto him that offereth it: it shall be an abomination, and the soul that eateth of it shall bear his iniquity [Lev. 7:15–18].

The peace offering was to be eaten at once. There was to be no delay. Thus, we are to stay very close to Christ for peace of conscience and for power over temptation. My friend, stay close to Christ! He gives peace only to those who are His own, to those who have entered into this glorious, wonderful fellowship with Him. We must look to Him and rest upon Him. When you find that Christ is adequate and wonderful, then the peace of God that passeth all understanding will enter into your heart. What a picture these sacrifices are of the Lord Jesus!

Now I am going to pick some verses out of the rest of the chapter.

And the flesh that toucheth any unclean thing shall not be eaten; it shall be burnt with fire: and as for the flesh, all that be clean shall eat thereof.

But the soul that eateth of the flesh of the sacrifice of peace offerings, that pertain unto the LORD, having his uncleanness upon him, even that soul shall be cut off from his people [Lev. 7:19-20].

An unclean person who ate of the peace offering was excommunicated. Even so today, there must be confession of sin on the part of the believer if he is to enter into fellowship with God.

And the LORD spake unto Moses, saying,

Speak unto the children of Israel, saying, Ye shall eat no manner of fat, of ox, or of sheep, or of goat.

Moreover ye shall eat no manner of blood, whether it be of fowl or of beast, in any of your dwellings.

Whatsoever soul it be that eateth any manner of blood, even that soul shall be cut off from his people [Lev. 7:22-23, 26-27].

We have already discussed the prohibition of eating blood. This is to remind us that man was redeemed by blood and that this is the basis and ground of our acceptance before God. They were also forbidden to eat the fat because the fat belonged to the Lord.

And the LORD spake unto Moses, saying,

Speak unto the children of Israel, saying, He that offereth the sacrifice of his peace offerings unto the LORD shall bring his oblation unto the LORD of the sacrifice of his peace offerings.

His own hands shall bring the offerings of the LORD made by fire, the fat with the breast, it shall he bring, that the breast may be waved for a wave offering before the LORD.

And the priest shall burn the fat upon the altar: but the breast shall be Aaron's and his sons'.

And the right shoulder shall ye give unto the priest for an heave offering of the sacrifices of your peace offerings.

He among the sons of Aaron, that offereth the blood of the peace offerings, and the fat, shall have the right shoulder for his part.

For the wave breast and the heave shoulder have I taken of the children of Israel from off the sacrifices of their peace offerings, and have given them unto Aaron the priest and unto his sons by a statute for ever from among the children of Israel [Lev. 7:28–34].

Aaron, his sons, and the priests received as their portion of the peace offering the breast and the shoulder. The breast speaks of the love of Christ for us. "But God commendeth his love toward us, in that, while we were yet sinners, Christ died for us" (Rom. 5:8). " . . . who loved me, and gave himself for me" (Gal. 2:20). " . . . having loved his own which were in the world, he loved them unto the end" (John 13:1).

The shoulder speaks of the power and strength of Christ. He is able to save to the uttermost. "My sheep hear my voice, and I know them, and they follow me: And I give unto them eternal life; and they shall never perish, neither shall any man pluck them out of my hand. My father, which gave them me, is greater than all; and no man is able to pluck them out of my Father's hand. I and my Father are one" (John 10:27–30).

He loves His own with an everlasting love and He can save to the uttermost. This is our portion in Christ!

All of these sacrifices in the Old Testament were not an end in themselves. The Old Testament saint was saved by faith just as we are saved by faith. "Offer the sacrifices of righteousness, and put your trust in the LORD" (Ps. 4:5). God was pleased when the sacrifices were brought in faith and in thanksgiving (Ps. 50:12–15 and 51:19). God was displeased when the sacrifices were brought as a dull routine and were polluted (Mal. 1:7–14).

All the sacrifices in the Old Testament demanded a more perfect antitype. This is found in Christ! "So Christ was once offered to bear the sins of many; and unto them that look for him shall he appear the second time without sin unto salvation" (Heb. 9:28).

This is the portion of the anointing of Aaron, and of the anointing of his sons, out of the offerings of the LORD made by fire, in the day when he presented them to minister unto the LORD in the priest's office;

Which the LORD commanded to be given them of the children of Israel, in the day that he anointed them, by a statute for ever throughout their generations.

This is the law of the burnt offering, of the meat offering, and of the sin offering, and of the trespass offering, and of the consecrations, and of the sacrifice of the peace offerings;

Which the LORD commanded Moses in mount Sinai, in the day that he commanded the children of Israel to offer their oblations unto the LORD, in the wilderness of Sinai [Lev. 7:35–38].

God sums up here the instructions given to Aaron and the priests in the law of the offerings of chapters 6 and 7.

CHAPTER 8

THEME: Calling of the congregation to witness the ritual of consecration of the priests; cleansing of Aaron and his sons; clothing of the high priest; consecration of the high priest; clothing and cleansing of the priests and Aaron; commandments given to Aaron and his sons

We come now to an altogether new section concerning the consecration of the priests. The consecration of the priests is important because it will throw a great deal of light on what is called consecration today in our churches. May I say that much of what we call consecration today is a pretty sorry substitute for the real article. "For the law maketh men high priests which have infirmity; but the word of the oath, which was since the law, maketh the Son, who is consecrated for evermore" (Heb. 7:28).

Our attention is now directed to the priests and not the sacrifices. We leave the brazen altar now and turn to the brazen laver. It was at the brazen altar that God dealt with the sin question for the sinner once and for all. But that doesn't mean that the saved sinner was perfect. He still sinned, unfortunately; so God must take him to the brazen laver where He washed him and kept him clean.

God still washes us and keeps us clean at the brazen laver. Jesus Christ is still girded with that towel of service and He washes us in the brazen laver of His blood and that keeps on cleansing us from all sin.

Israel had a priesthood and this was written for them. In fact, the Book of Leviticus really is written for the Levites. It was God's original intention to make the entire nation of Israel a kingdom of priests. "And ye shall be unto me a kingdom of priests, and an holy nation . . ." (Exod. 19:6). Their sin in the matter of the golden calf prevented this. Instead, only one tribe was taken, the tribe of Levi. Out of this tribe only one man was chosen as the high priest and that was Aaron.

The church today is a priesthood, and Christ is the great High Priest. " . . . We have such an high priest, who is set on the right hand of the throne of the Majesty in the heavens" (Heb. 8:1). "But ye are a chosen generation, a royal priesthood, an holy nation, a peculiar people; that ye should shew forth the praises of him who hath called you out of darkness into his marvelous light" (1 Pet. 2:9). "And hast made us unto our God kings and priests: and we shall reign on the earth" (Rev. 5:10). "And hath made us kings and priests unto God and his Father; to him be glory and dominion for ever and ever. Amen" (Rev. 1:6). "We have an altar, whereof they have no right to eat which serve the tabernacle" (Heb. 13:10). That altar today is in heaven. It is at the throne of grace.

In the future, after the church is gone, I believe that the nation Israel will be the priests on the earth during the Millennium.

The definition of a priest was not left to man's invention but is explained in the Scripture. "For every high priest taken from among men is ordained for men in things pertaining to God, that he may offer both gifts and sacrifices for sins" (Heb. 5:1). Priesthood in the Scriptures bears no similarity to any order of priests in any religion at the present time.

A priest is one who represents man before God. He goes in to God on behalf of man. He is the opposite of a prophet. A prophet comes out from God, to speak for God, to man. A priest comes out from man and goes to God, to speak for man to God, and to represent man.

You can see that the Lord Jesus is both Prophet and Priest. He came out from God and spoke for God to man. He reveals God to man. Now He has gone from man back to God and is our great High Priest. He represents us there. In fact, we are in Him! My friend, if you are not in Him, then you are not up there. You and I could never get there on our own.

A knowledge of the tabernacle is essential to an understanding of the Book of Leviticus and especially of the priesthood. The typology of the tabernacle and of the priesthood is so rich in meaning and detail that there is a danger of emphasizing one facet to the exclusion of another and thereby giving a wrong inference. I do think we need to note that the outer court of the tabernacle represents the world down here.

This is where Christ bled and died. The Holy Place is the unseen to which our great High Priest has gone.

Actually, this is what happened when the Lord Jesus died on the Cross and then went back up to heaven. He took the tabernacle and the meaning of it, which was horizontal here on the earth, and He made it perpendicular. That is, the altar is down here—this is where He died on the Cross. The Holy Place is up there, and He is even now in the Holy of Holies. Listen to these passages which explain this. "Seeing then that we have a great high priest, that is passed into the heavens, Jesus the Son of God, let us hold fast our profession" (Heb. 4:14). "But Christ being come an high priest of good things to come, by a greater and more perfect tabernacle, not made with hands, that is to say, not of this building" (Heb. 9:11). "Now of the things which we have spoken this is the sum: we have such an high priest, who is set on the right hand of the throne of the Majesty in the heavens; a minister of the sanctuary, and of the true tabernacle, which the Lord pitched, and not man" (Heb. 8:1-2). "It was therefore necessary that the patterns of things in the heavens should be purified with these; but the heavenly things themselves with better sacrifices than these. For Christ is not entered into the holy places made with hands, which are the figures of the true; but into heaven itself, now to appear in the presence of God for us" (Heb. 9:23-24).

He is up yonder today. I wish we could bring this reality into our faith. We attend church and go through a little ritual and often the realities of our faith are forgotten. He is up yonder, friend, right now. You are to approach God through Him. We are told to come with boldness. He appears now in the presence of God for us. My friend, you are not alone down here. There is availability with God through Christ. The tabernacle is now perpendicular and the Holy of Holies is in heaven.

Twelve times in this chapter it is stated that the Lord commanded Moses. The final clincher is the last verse, "So Aaron and his sons did all things which the Lord commanded by the hand of Moses" (Lev. 8:36). These are the things which God commanded. Consecration must be the way He says it is to be done!

Some people believe in a late dating of the Book of Leviticus as the invention of the priesthood. Yet it says here that this was all done as God commanded it. Do you believe in the inspired Word of God? Then you cannot accept the late dating of Leviticus, but believe the inerrancy of Scripture and that this was done at the command of God.

CALLING OF THE CONGREGATION
TO WITNESS THE RITUAL

And the LORD spake unto Moses, saying,

Take Aaron and his sons with him, and the garments, and the anointing oil, and a bullock for the sin offering, and two rams, and a basket of unleavened bread;

And gather thou all the congregation together unto the door of the tabernacle of the congregation [Lev. 8:1–3].

Moses is commanded to bring Aaron and his sons, with all the articles which are to be used in the consecration of the priests, to the door of the tabernacle. This sounds somewhat like a grocery list, but every item it mentions is very important.

Then he is to gather the congregation together to witness the ritual of consecrating the priests. This is to be a very impressive service. They will see that God takes feeble men and sets them aside for His service. I feel like saying a hallelujah to that because He will do that for you and for me. "For the law maketh men high priests which have infirmity; but the word of the oath, which was since the law, maketh the Son, who is consecrated for evermore" (Heb. 7:28). Christ was really consecrated. In a sense no one else is really consecrated. But the marvelous thing is that God will accept men with infirmities. If He demanded perfection, we would all be left out. Thank God, He takes them as they are, infirm.

And Moses did as the Lord commanded him; and the assembly was gathered together unto the door of the tabernacle of the congregation.

And Moses said unto the congregation, This is the thing which the LORD commanded to be done [Lev. 8:4–5].

Moses does what he is commanded to do. The people likewise obey and come together for this service. Moses gives a word of explanation that he is following the instructions of the Lord in all that he does.

CLEANSING OF AARON AND HIS SONS

And Moses brought Aaron and his sons, and washed them with water [Lev. 8:6].

Moses brings Aaron and his sons to the laver for washing. He gives them a bath, if you please. This signifies that they are to be holy, pure, and clean if they are to serve the Lord. They have already been to the altar for forgiveness, but they need cleansing.

A great many people today say that they are qualified for service because they are saved. Now it is true that salvation is the prime requisite, but for service one must also be cleansed. You must be cleansed to be used! Listen to these verses from Scripture:

"Not by works of righteousness which we have done, but according to his mercy he saved us, by the washing of regeneration, and renewing of the Holy Ghost" (Titus 3:5). "Let us draw near with a true heart in full assurance of faith, having our hearts sprinkled from an evil conscience, and our bodies washed with pure water" (Heb. 10:22). "That he might sanctify and cleanse it with the washing of water by the word" (Eph. 5:26). "Jesus saith to him, He that is washed needeth not save to wash his feet, but is clean every whit: and ye are clean, but not all" (John 13:10). "If we confess our sins, he is faithful and just to forgive us our sins, and to cleanse us from all unrighteousness" (1 John 1:9).

The Holy Ghost renews us as we go along, but we need a washing from the Lord. With what does He wash us? What is the cleansing agent? It is the Word of God. That is what cleanses us. The Lord said that His disciples needed to be washed because their feet were dirty. They all had a bath; that is, they all had been saved (except Judas), but they still needed their feet washed so that they might have fellowship with Him. This cleansing is for service.

How do we get that washing? It is by *confession* that we are forgiven and cleansed. Do you want to be used of God? Then go confess your sins, dear Christian. That is the first step. This is God's way. This is His command. We either must do it His way or we cannot be of service. He has His way of doing things and we need to learn and obey His ways.

CLOTHING OF THE HIGH PRIEST

And he put upon him the coat, and girded him with the girdle, and clothed him with the robe, and put the ephod upon him, and he girded him with the curious girdle of the ephod, and bound it unto him therewith [Lev. 8:7].

The clothing of the high priest is a picture of our great High Priest in all His extraordinary graces and glory. Each article of clothing was symbolic. There were eight articles worn by the high priest. Four were the same or similar to those worn by all the priests. Four were peculiar to him, and separated him from the other priests. They were garments for glory and for beauty.

The four which were common to all the priests were as follows: the coat, the girdle, the turban or mitre or bonnet, and the breeches. These were all made of white linen, with the exception of the turban. The white linen speaks of righteousness. Every believer is clothed in the righteousness of Christ. It is essential for service to be thus clothed, and to be girded is necessary for active obedience. The coat and girdle mentioned in this verse were the basic garments which all the priests wore. These garments are described in detail in Exodus 28.

And he put the breastplate upon him: also he put in the breastplate the Urim and the Thummim [Lev. 8:8].

The breastplate is also described in Exodus 28. The Urim and Thummim were placed in the breastplate. *Urim* means "light" and *Thummim* means "perfections," so these were the lights and perfections. I do not know exactly how they functioned. Some think that they had to do with the Law and that possibly the Law was written on stones. In Psalm 19 there is a reference to this. "The law of the LORD is perfect, [perfections—Thummim], converting the soul: the testimony of the LORD is sure, making wise the simple" (Ps. 19:7). "The statutes of the LORD are right, rejoicing the heart: the commandment of the LORD is pure, enlightening the eyes [light—Urim]" (Ps. 19:8). Apparently the Urim and Thummin had something to do with determining the will of God. There is a spiritual application for us. We need the Word of God today, and we need the leading of God to determine the will of God in our lives.

> **And he put the mitre upon his head; also upon the mitre, even upon his forefront, did he put the golden plate, the holy crown; as the LORD commanded Moses [Lev. 8:9].**

The mitre of the high priest had put upon it the golden crown described in Exodus 28. Remember that graven upon it was HOLINESS TO THE LORD. These garments distinguished the high priest from the other priests. They set forth the glories and beauties of our great High Priest who died down here to save us and lives at God's right hand to keep us saved. "For if, when we were enemies, we were reconciled, we shall be saved by his life" (Rom. 5:10). ". . . because I live, ye shall live also" (John 14:19).

The sons of Aaron were at his side clothed in simple linen. This is a picture of our great High Priest with His many sons who are being gathered with Him and who are clothed in His righteousness. "For it became him, for whom are all things, and by whom are all things, in bringing many sons unto glory, to make the captain of their salvation perfect through sufferings" (Heb. 2:10). We come to Christ as lost sinners and He covers us with His righteousness.

The priest carried stones on each shoulder with six of the names of the twelve tribes on each shoulder. The twelve stones on the breastplate had a name of each of the tribes on each, one tribe on each stone. The great high priest carried the nation of Israel on his shoulder and upon his heart. The shoulder speaks of strength and the heart speaks of love.

CONSECRATION OF THE HIGH PRIEST

And Moses took the anointing oil, and anointed the tabernacle and all that was therein, and sanctified them [Lev. 8:10].

The tabernacle and all the vessels of the ministry had been sprinkled with blood (Heb. 9:21). Now they are anointed with oil. They were already redeemed and cleansed by the blood. Now they are anointed with the oil which symbolizes the Holy Spirit. Now the Holy Spirit is free to move and work in the worship and service of the tabernacle. "God is a Spirit: and they that worship him must worship him in spirit and in truth" (John 4:24).

And he sprinkled thereof upon the altar seven times, and anointed the altar and all his vessels, both the laver and his foot, to sanctify them.

And he poured of the anointing oil upon Aaron's head, and anointed him, to sanctify him [Lev. 8:11–12].

The act of sprinkling the oil speaks of sanctification. All was now ready for use, having been set apart for the service of God. Aaron was not sprinkled but anointed with the oil. He was just covered with oil! "It is like the precious ointment upon the head, that ran down upon the beard, even Aaron's beard: that went down to the skirts of his garments" (Ps. 133:2).

Just so the Holy Spirit (of whom oil is the symbol) was poured out upon Christ at His baptism. It is distinctly stated that ". . . God giveth not the Spirit by *measure* unto him" (John 3:34). In other words, God gives the Holy Spirit to His Son without measure.

It must be noted that the oil was poured on Aaron before the priests had the blood applied to them. Our High Priest needed no offering for sin. We do; He did not. "Thou hast loved righteousness, and hated iniquity; therefore God, even thy God, hath anointed thee with the oil of gladness above thy fellows" (Heb. 1:9).

CLOTHING OF THE PRIESTS

And Moses brought Aaron's sons, and put coats upon them, and girded them with girdles, and put bonnets upon them; as the LORD commanded Moses [Lev. 8:13].

We are told again that this was all done according to the commandment of the Lord. This reminds us once more that we must stand clothed in the righteousness of Christ.

CLEANSING OF THE PRIESTS AND AARON

And he brought the bullock for the sin offering: and Aaron and his sons laid their hands upon the head of the bullock for the sin offering [Lev. 8:14].

The bullock was the sin offering for the high priest. The four sons of Aaron could claim it as their offering, too. Their sins are transferred to the victim. That is understood by the laying on of hands. God wrote indelibly in their souls and burned it into their hearts that they were sinners, even though they were in the service of God.

You will find as you go through the Word of God that God's men have always been conscious of the fact that they are sinners. "For innumerable evils have compassed me about: mine iniquities have taken hold upon me, so that I am not able to look up; they are more than the hairs of mine head: therefore my heart faileth me" (Ps. 40:12). Friend, do you feel that you are that kind of a sinner? God can do something for you if you are like that. After all, if you don't get sick enough to go to the doctor, you won't go to him. If you aren't sure that you are a real sinner, you are not apt to go to Christ. "For mine iniquities are gone over mine head: as an heavy burden they are too heavy for me" (Ps. 38:4).

Friends, if you have a load that is too heavy for you, get someone else to carry it for you. There is Someone who says, "Come unto me all ye that labor and are heavy laden. I will give you rest. I'll take your burdens." And don't try to fool God. He knows all about you; so you might just as well tell Him the whole story.

And he slew it; and Moses took the blood, and put it
upon the horns of the altar round about with his finger,
and purified the altar, and poured the blood at the bottom of the altar, and sanctified it, to make reconciliation
upon it.

And he took all the fat that was upon the inwards, and
the caul above the liver, and the two kidneys, and their
fat, and Moses burned it upon the altar.

But the bullock, and his hide, his flesh, and his dung, he
burnt with fire without the camp; as the LORD commanded Moses [Lev. 8:15–17].

This ritual is meaningless until we understand the spiritual lesson.
They follow the ritual of the sin offering with the exception that the
blood is put on the horns of the brazen altar rather than on the golden
altar. Even the altar which is used for the bloody sacrifices must be
dedicated with blood. This is to remind us that there is no merit in the
wood of the cross. There are a lot of people today who feel there is
some merit in the cross itself. There is no merit in the cross! *The merit
is in the One who shed His blood for us there.* Though He became sin
for us, He was not polluted with sin. He was not stained with sin. He
was "made sin" and yet He was "separate from sinners." Again, we
notice that all this was done at the commandment of God.

And he brought the ram for the burnt offering: and
Aaron and his sons laid their hands upon the head of
the ram.

And he killed it; and Moses sprinkled the blood upon
the altar round about.

And he cut the ram into pieces; and Moses burnt the
head, and the pieces, and the fat.

And he washed the inwards and the legs in water; and
Moses burnt the whole ram upon the altar: it was a

burnt sacrifice for a sweet savour, and an offering made by fire unto the LORD; as the LORD commanded Moses [Lev. 8:18–21].

They now go through the ritual of the burnt offering. The burnt offering followed the sin offering. It is impossible to comprehend the beauties and merits of Christ until the sin question has been dealt with in a manner satisfactory to God. The sin offering represents what Christ did for us on the Cross. The burnt offering represents who He is. You can never really know Him until you come to Him first to save you and you accept Him as your substitute for sin. He paid the penalty for your sin. That is of prime importance to know.

Actually, *fellowship* in the New Testament means to share the things of Christ. Only those who are the blood-bought believers can share the things of Christ. The priests had to go inside the holy place to see the beauties of that place. The outside was not very pretty. Just so, the unbelieving world does not see the beauty of Christ and rejects Him, but the child of God is finding new beauties and glories in Him every day.

And he brought the other ram, the ram of consecration: and Aaron and his sons laid their hands upon the head of the ram.

And he slew it; and Moses took of the blood of it, and put it upon the tip of Aaron's right ear, and upon the thumb of his right hand, and upon the great toe of his right foot.

And he brought Aaron's sons and Moses put of the blood upon the tip of their right ear, and upon the thumbs of their right hands, and upon the great toes of their right feet: and Moses sprinkled the blood upon the altar round about [Lev. 8:22–24].

The ram of consecration was actually a trespass offering. No peace offerings were made. Why not? Because the priests were already in the sanctuary, the place of fellowship and communion.

The blood-tipped ear symbolizes the ear that will hear the voice of God. Without that, friend, you are not going to hear Him. The natural man does not receive the things of Christ. The blood-tipped hand was essential for service. It is impossible to serve the Lord before one is saved. The blood-tipped foot was essential for the walk before God. All of this is symbolic of the fact that the *total* personality must be presented to God.

> **And he took the fat, and the rump, and all the fat that was upon the inwards, and the caul above the liver, and the two kidneys, and their fat, and the right shoulder:**

> **And out of the basket of unleavened bread, that was before the Lord, he took one unleavened cake, and a cake of oiled bread, and one wafer, and put them on the fat, and upon the right shoulder:**

> **And he put all upon Aaron's hands, and upon his sons' hands, and waved them for a wave offering before the Lord.**

> **And Moses took them from off their hands, and burnt them on the altar upon the burnt offering: they were consecrations for a sweet savour: it is an offering made by fire unto the Lord.**

> **And Moses took the breast, and waved it for a wave offering before the Lord: for of the ram of consecration it was Moses' part; as the Lord commanded Moses [Lev. 8:25–29].**

These verses tell that they took parts from all the offerings and put them together and placed them in the hands of Aaron and his sons. They then waved them before the Lord. This was total commitment to God on the basis of the value of one offering. "So Christ was once offered to bear the sins of many; and unto them that look for him shall he appear the second time without sin unto salvation" (Heb. 9:28).

And Moses took of the anointing oil, and of the blood which was upon the altar, and sprinkled it upon Aaron, and upon his garments, and upon his sons, and upon his sons' garments with him; and sanctified Aaron, and his garments, and his sons, and his sons' garments with him [Lev. 8:30].

Now the priests together with Aaron are consecrated with blood and oil. Blood is for the forgiveness of sins, the work of Christ; the oil is for the anointing of the Spirit of God. (The instructions for this were given in Exodus 29:21.) This speaks of the Lord Jesus who said, "And for their sakes I sanctify myself, that they also might be sanctified through the truth" (John 17:19).

This should also remind us that believers are to walk before the world as the blood-bought children of God. This is what Jude meant: "And others save with fear, pulling them out of the fire; hating even the garment spotted by the flesh" (Jude 23). You see, we can go through consecration services and make promises of consecration, but the real question is what your neighbors think about you. What do the folk where you go to school think of you? Do the people with whom you work think that you are serving God? Do they think you are consecrated?

I heard a wonderful thing about a Christian the other day. An unsaved man said, "I don't know much about that fellow's religion, but if I ever get religion, I want his kind." I'm afraid that too often what the world sees of the Christian is not really very appealing. Our life should be so that it would attract the man out in the world to the Lord Jesus Christ.

COMMANDMENTS GIVEN TO AARON AND HIS SONS

And Moses said unto Aaron and to his sons, Boil the flesh at the door of the tabernacle of the congregation: and there eat it with the bread that is in the basket of consecrations, as I commanded, saying, Aaron and his sons shall eat it.

And that which remaineth of the flesh and of the bread shall ye burn with fire [Lev. 8:31–32].

I told you at the beginning of this section that this sounds like a grocery list, and this is how this section on consecration ends. They are to eat the food that is left. This typifies the fact that believers are now to feed upon the finished work of Christ. Peace and satisfaction are the portion of the believers only in ratio to the measure in which they feed on Christ. Nothing is to be left. All must be consumed or burnt with fire. Nothing is to be left to spoil or waste. Oh, how God's people need to feed upon Him!

And ye shall not go out of the door of the tabernacle of the congregation in seven days, until the days of your consecration be at an end: for seven days shall he consecrate you.

As he hath done this day, so the LORD hath commanded to do, to make an atonement for you.

Therefore shall ye abide at the door of the tabernacle of the congregation day and night seven days, and keep the charge of the LORD, that ye die not: for so I am commanded.

So Aaron and his sons did all things which the LORD commanded by the hand of Moses [Lev. 8:33–36].

There were to be seven days of consecration and meditation. They were to remain continually on duty at the door of the tabernacle. So it is with our great High Priest who ever lives to make intercession for His own. You may wake up at 2:00 A.M., and He is right up there for you. You may be out in a difficult and dark place, but He is right up there for you. He is always available!

All this was done at the commandment of God. This is emphasized, as it is repeated in each of the last three verses of this chapter. The reason for this will be made clear in the next chapter.

CHAPTER 9

THEME: Aaron prepares to begin his service; Aaron offers the sin offering; Aaron offers the burnt offering; Aaron offers the meal and peace offerings; Aaron blesses the people and the glory of the Lord appears

This chapter is intensely interesting, as it not only marks the initiation of Aaron and his sons into the service of the priesthood, but it gives in detail the daily ritual of the service of the priests. With the exception of the great Day of Atonement, very little detail is given in the remainder of Scripture relative to the daily ritual.

This marks the time when the priest for the first time became a priest. Although one was born in Aaron's line, he was not fully a priest until he was consecrated. The Hebrew word for consecration literally means "to fill the hand." That means we come to God with empty hands. Consecration isn't a promise to go out as a missionary or to do something else for the Lord. Consecration means to come to the Lord with empty hands and ask, "Lord, what will You have me to do?" *He* does the filling! That is consecration.

Too many folk think they must bring something to God if they are to be consecrated. Some folk seem to think they are giving the Lord a whole lot if they give themselves. We're not giving Him very much, friends. When He got me, all He got was just so much sin. That's all.

The Septuagint adopted the Greek word *teleioo* to express consecration. This expresses the same thought. *Telos* means "end," and it means "the purpose," meaning to accomplish what God wants you to accomplish. It means to fulfill the end for which you were born. We were born for the purpose of completing the body of Christ. And He was born for the purpose of coming down here to accomplish the will of God in order that He might bring us home to glory. "For it became him, for whom are all things, and by whom are all things, in bringing many sons unto glory, to make the captain of their salvation perfect through sufferings" (Heb. 2:10). You see, Jesus was consecrated. He had a purpose. "For the law maketh men high priests which have in-firmity; but the word of the oath, which was since the law, maketh the Son, who is consecrated for evermore" (Heb. 7:28).

In this chapter it is the office of Jesus, not His character, which is in view. It is Jesus accomplishing the purpose, the God-given purpose, in His office.

AARON PREPARES TO BEGIN HIS SERVICE

And it came to pass on the eighth day, that Moses called Aaron and his sons, and the elders of Israel;

And he said unto Aaron, Take thee a young calf for a sin offering, and a ram for a burnt offering, without blemish, and offer them before the Lord [Lev. 9:1–2].

All of this was done at the commandment of God. They had carried out the details of the seven days and now, on the eighth day, Aaron was to begin his service as the high priest. The eighth day is the first day of the week! That is the day that Jesus came back from the dead. Christ entered into His office as High Priest after His death and resurrection.

Hebrews 8:4 and 9:10–12 tell us that if Christ were on earth, He would not be a priest. It was after He ascended into heaven that He became High Priest in the tabernacle not made with hands, up in heaven. By His own blood He entered into the Holy Place.

As Aaron entered into his office as high priest on the first day of the week, his four sons were there as witnesses. Likewise, we have four Gospels which bear witness to the fact of the death and resurrection of Christ. We today have a perfect and complete Priest. "And being made perfect, he became the author of eternal salvation unto all them that obey him" (Heb. 5:9). We obey Him when we believe Him and believe on Him. We obey Him, after we are believers, when we attempt to do His will. That is consecration, friends. We come to him empty; we hold out our empty hands and ask Christ to fill us.

Aaron was not our great High Priest. He needed to make a sin offering for himself. The high priest on all great public occasions began by making an offering for himself. By this he was declaring that he was not the Christ but that there would be One who comes after him. He would be the great High Priest—"Who needeth not daily, as those high priests, to offer up sacrifice, first for his own sins, and then for the people's: for this he did once, when he offered up himself" (Heb. 7:27).

> **And unto the children of Israel thou shalt speak, saying, Take ye a kid of the goats for a sin offering; and a calf and a lamb, both of the first year, without blemish, for a burnt offering;**
>
> **Also a bullock and a ram for peace offerings, to sacrifice before the Lord; and a meat offering mingled with oil: for today the Lord will appear unto you [Lev. 9:3–4].**

Aaron was commanded to have the people bring all the offerings to God with the exception of the trespass offering. At the very beginning there was no need for the trespass offering because they had not had time to commit a trespass. They offered the regular kid of the goats for the sin offering; a double offering of a calf and a lamb for the burnt offering; a double offering of a bullock and a ram for the peace offering; and the regular meal offering. The glory of the Lord was to appear to them that day. This was to show that through the death of Christ, on to the resurrected High Priest at God's right hand, is the way we approach God.

> **And they brought that which Moses commanded before the tabernacle of the congregation: and all the congregation drew near and stood before the Lord.**
>
> **And Moses said, This is the thing which the Lord commanded that ye should do: and the glory of the Lord shall appear unto you.**
>
> **And Moses said unto Aaron, Go unto the altar, and offer thy sin offering, and thy burnt offering, and make an atonement for thyself, and for the people: and offer the offering of the people, and make an atonement for them; as the Lord commanded [Lev. 9:5–7].**

The people obey, and Moses assures them that the glory of the Lord will appear to them.

AARON OFFERS THE SIN OFFERING

Aaron therefore went unto the altar, and slew the calf of the sin offering, which was for himself.

And the sons of Aaron brought the blood unto him: and he dipped his finger in the blood, and put it upon the horns of the altar, and poured out the blood at the bottom of the altar.

But the fat, and the kidneys, and the caul above the liver of the sin offering, he burnt upon the altar; as the LORD commanded Moses.

And the flesh and the hide he burnt with fire without the camp [Lev. 9:8–11].

These verses describe how Aaron carried out the ritual of the sin offering in meticulous detail. The sin offering was made first. Why? When the offerings were first presented, the burnt offering was first and the sin offering came last. Well, you see, the offerings were first presented from God's viewpoint. But now we are approaching God from man's viewpoint. Man comes to God as a sinner. You and I, my friend, come as sinners. It is the sin question which must be settled first. "In whom we have redemption through his blood, the forgiveness of sins, according to the riches of his grace" (Eph. 1:7).

AARON OFFERS THE BURNT OFFERING

The ritual for the burnt offering was followed in meticulous detail. First Aaron offered for himself.

And he slew the burnt offering: and Aaron's sons presented unto him the blood, which he sprinkled round about upon the altar.

> And they presented the burnt offering unto him, with the pieces thereof, and the head: and he burnt them upon the altar.
>
> And he did wash the inwards and the legs, and burnt them upon the burnt offering on the altar [Lev. 9:12–14].

The sin offering and the burnt offering for the people were then presented.

> And he brought the people's offering, and took the goat, which was the sin offering for the people, and slew it, and offered it for sin, as the first.
>
> And he brought the burnt offering, and offered it according to the manner [Lev. 9:15–16].

All of this is a picture of Christ. "Yet it pleased the LORD to bruise him; he hath put him to grief: when thou shalt make his soul an offering for sin, he shall see his seed, he shall prolong his days, and the pleasure of the LORD shall prosper in his hand" (Isa. 53:10). "For he hath made him to be sin for us, who knew no sin; that we might be made the righteousness of God in him" (2 Cor. 5:21).

The sin offering is made sin. Christ had the sin of the world pressed down upon Him as one great globe, a whole world, of sin.

AARON OFFERS THE MEAL AND PEACE OFFERINGS

> And he brought the meat offering, and took an handful thereof, and burnt it upon the altar, beside the burnt sacrifice of the morning.
>
> He slew also the bullock and the ram for a sacrifice of peace offerings, which was for the people: and Aaron's sons presented unto him the blood, which he sprinkled upon the altar round about,
>
> And the fat of the bullock and of the ram, the rump, and that which covereth the inwards, and the kidneys, and the caul above the liver:

And they put the fat upon the breasts, and he burnt the
fat upon the altar:

And the breasts and the right shoulder Aaron waved for
a wave offering before the LORD; as Moses commanded
[Lev. 9:17-21].

The meal offering followed the regular ritual. The same is true for the
peace offering. Aaron, as the representative for the nation, presents
the sacrifices before the Lord through the shedding of the blood. The
people are accepted. Blessing will follow.

AARON BLESSES THE PEOPLE AND
THE GLORY OF THE LORD APPEARS

And Aaron lifted up his hand toward the people, and
blessed them, and came down from offering of the sin
offering, and the burnt offering, and peace offerings.

And Moses and Aaron went into the tabernacle of the
congregation, and came out, and blessed the people:
and the glory of the LORD appeared unto all the people.

And there came a fire out from before the LORD, and consumed upon the altar the burnt offering and the fat:
which when all the people saw, they shouted, and fell on
their faces [Lev. 9:22-24].

Blessing follows the offering of the three offerings: the sin offering,
the burnt offering, and the peace offering. Then Moses and Aaron re-
tired into the tabernacle. It is thought that at the time of the evening
sacrifice they came forth to bless the people and then the glory of the
Lord appeared. All is complete now. The people shout and fall on
their faces in adoration and praise.

Christ is now entered into the Holy Place, which is in heaven itself,
to appear there for you and me today. Oh, my friend, lay hold of this
living Christ. Fall before Him in adoration and praise.

CHAPTER 10

THEME: Incident concerning Nadab and Abihu, sons
of Aaron; instructions coming out of the incident;
injunctions concerning the offerings in connection
with the incident

The Book of Leviticus has very little narrative, but is filled with
instructions, rituals, regulations, and laws. This chapter offers a
change of pace in the reading for it is a narrative. However, the interest
is almost obliterated because it is a horrible tragedy which is recorded
here.

This is another blot on man's long and sordid history of sin and
willfulness. It is the record of the rebellion and disobedience of the
two sons of Aaron. It follows the glorious day of dedication recorded
in the preceding chapter. So often we find this happening. After a
flush of victory, there is defeat—as in the Book of Joshua, the victory of
Jericho is followed by the ignoble defeat of Ai.

The presumption of Nadab and Abihu is frightening in the light of
the clear teaching which God gave at Sinai. "And let the priests also,
which come near to the Lord, sanctify themselves, lest the Lord break
forth upon them" (Exod. 19:22). In Exodus 30:34–38 God gave to
Moses the formula for the incense to be used in the tabernacle and
said, "As for the perfume which thou shalt make, ye shall not make to
yourselves according to the composition thereof: it shall be unto thee
holy for the Lord. Whosoever shall make like unto that, to smell
thereto, shall even be cut off from his people" (Exod. 30:37–38).

The holiness of God is set forth at the beginning of the age of law
by this incident. The holiness of God is set forth at the beginning of
the age of grace by the incident concerning Ananias and Sapphira.
Death was the drastic penalty in both cases. Our God is holy, and He
deals with His children on that level. "For our God is a consuming
fire" (Heb. 12:29) is something we all need to learn today. "Knowing
therefore the terror of the Lord, we persuade men . . ." (2 Cor. 5:11).
This is something we need to recognize today.

There is a warning in Hebrews 12:25: "See that ye refuse not him that speaketh. For if they escaped not who refused him that spake on earth, much more shall not we escape, if we turn away from him that speaketh from heaven." This is one of the great sins of the hour. People are not hearing what God has to say in His Word.

INCIDENT CONCERNING NADAB AND ABIHU, SONS OF AARON

And Nadab and Abihu, the sons of Aaron, took either of them his censer, and put fire therein, and put incense thereon, and offered strange fire before the LORD, which he commanded them not.

And there went out fire from the LORD, and devoured them, and they died before the LORD [Lev. 10:1-2].

It may be argued that the penalty of death was too severe for the transgression committed. But notice particularly what God says here, "Which he commanded them not." This reveals something of the enormity for the crime, and therefore the penalty is just. This was willful and deliberate disobedience to the expressed command of God.

Precisely what did they do which brought down such severe judgment upon them? This act has been called "will-worship" and that is what it is. What did they do wrong? I'd like to make three suggestions:

1. They probably did not light the censer of incense from coals from off the altar, which was the fire which had come down from heaven. It apparently was understood that this must be done. This was the practice on the great Day of Atonement as is clearly stated in Leviticus 16:12: "And he shall take a censer full of burning coals of fire from off the altar before the LORD, and his hands full of sweet incense beaten small, and bring it within the veil." This was the same ritual followed at the time of the rebellion of Korah (Num. 16:46). It

must be assumed that this method was the only correct one. The ritual they followed was contrary to God's way.

2. Their timing was out of step with the God-given ritual. The ritual for the day had been completed. They should have consulted Aaron in this matter. Apparently, they wanted to repeat the marvelous display of the preceding chapter. Isn't this a problem today, when with our will-worship we try to duplicate what God has done? There are many who try to duplicate the experience of the day of Pentecost. God is sovereign! His will must be followed even as to the timing. The Spirit of God will move according to His own will. We should simply make ourselves available and obedient to Him.

3. Others have supposed that they intruded beyond the veil which was expressly forbidden. There is justification for their viewpoint as stated in Leviticus 16:1-2: "And the Lord spake unto Moses after the death of the two sons of Aaron, when they offered before the Lord, and died; and the Lord said unto Moses, Speak unto Aaron thy brother, that he come not at all times into the holy place within the veil before the mercy seat, which is upon the ark; that he die not: for I will appear in the cloud upon the mercy seat."

It would seem that this prohibition came out of the incident of Nadab and Abihu. They were wrong as to the place they should come. God had commanded them as to the manner, the time, and the place. They were wrong in all three.

Some may still think that God surely uses extreme surgery. It *does* reveal that our God is a jealous God. He is sovereign in all His dealings, and those who come to Him must come on His terms. It is still true that to obey is better than sacrifice. God will not accept worship in our own will, no matter how sincere. We need to note here, too, that the high position of these men offered them no immunity.

The sudden execution of judgment here is startling. There is no escaping the statement that the fire was from the Lord. Let us recognize that judgment is not foreign to the age of grace. It may not always be this sudden. "For this cause many are weak and sickly among you, and many sleep" (1 Cor. 11:30). In the case of Ananias and Sapphira it was just as sudden and sure.

This does not mean that the believer in Christ can lose his salvation! Nadab and Abihu, and Ananias and Sapphira did not lose their salvation. Neither did the believers in the Corinthian congregation. This is made very clear. "For if we would judge ourselves, we should not be judged. But when we are judged, we are chastened of the Lord, that we should not be condemned with the world" (1 Cor. 11:31–32).

Physical death is oftentimes a judgment for the child of God. There is a sin unto death (1 John 5:16) but it is physical death. The child of God is not condemned with the world. These judgments in both the Old and New Testaments are examples to believers that will-worship is detestable to God. The believer must come to God in God's way. The believing sinner must worship God's way.

Hebrews 10:19–22 tells us very definitely that we are to come to God with boldness, but that it must be by the blood of Jesus. We come because we have a High Priest over the house of God. We are to come ". . . with a true heart in full assurance of faith, having our hearts sprinkled from an evil conscience, and our bodies washed with pure water." God makes a difference! "And that ye may put difference between holy and unholy, and between unclean and clean" (Lev. 10:10). Don't get the idea that God can't move in with judgment today.

Let me get very personal. A friend of mine, who knows me very well, said, "McGee, since you have had cancer and you know you still have cancer in your body now, did it ever occur to you that maybe it is a judgment from God?" I told this brother, "You know, I have waked up in the stillness and darkness of the night and I've thought just that, and I have cried out to God." May I say to you, I don't exclude myself. If we don't judge ourselves, God will judge us, so that we are not condemned with the world! God does all things well! When I say these things to you, remember that I am going through it. This fellow knows what he is talking about.

What an illustration this is that sometimes Jesus will come in fiery judgment upon the lost world. Enoch preached this! Enoch prophesied, ". . . Behold, the Lord cometh with ten thousands of his saints, to execute judgment upon all, and to convince all that are ungodly among them of all their ungodly deeds which they have ungodly committed, and of all their hard speeches which ungodly sinners have spoken against him" (Jude 14–15). Peter said the same thing. "And if the righteous scarcely be saved, where shall the ungodly and the sinner appear?" (1 Pet. 4:18).

> **Then Moses said unto Aaron, This is it that the LORD spake, saying, I will be sanctified in them that come nigh me, and before all the people I will be glorified. And Aaron held his peace.**
>
> **And Moses called Mishael and Elzaphan, the sons of Uzziel the uncle of Aaron, and said unto them, Come near, carry your brethren from before the sanctuary out of the camp.**
>
> **So they went near, and carried them in their coats out of the camp; as Moses had said [Lev. 10:3–5].**

When the news spread throughout the hosts of Israel, the people must have gathered about the tabernacle to view the dead bodies of these young men. Moses quoted the words of the Lord to give them an explanation for the judgment. "And let the priests also, which come near to the LORD, sanctify themselves, lest the LORD break forth upon them" (Exod. 19:22).

Those who have been brought into a particular nearness to God must exercise a sharp insight into the holiness and the righteous demands of God. "You only have I known of all the families of the earth: therefore I will punish you for all your iniquities" (Amos 3:2). As God judged His people Israel, so God judges His saints today in order that the world may know He is a holy God.

Aaron's attitude and conduct are noticeable. He maintains a demeanor of silence. There is no cry of disappointment, grief, or resentment toward God. He bows in heartbroken submission to the will of God. His grief must have been deep, but he can say nothing against the sovereign will of God. You notice God says, "I will be sanctified in them that come nigh me."

Moses called upon two of the priests who were cousins of the slain men to remove the dead bodies from before the sanctuary. As the people looked on in awe, they were carried out of the camp.

INSTRUCTIONS COMING OUT OF THE INCIDENT

And Moses said unto Aaron, and unto Eleazar and unto Ithamar, his sons, Uncover not your heads, neither rend your clothes; lest ye die, and lest wrath come upon all the people: but let your brethren, the whole house of Israel, bewail the burning which the LORD hath kindled.

And ye shall not go out from the door of the tabernacle of the congregation, lest ye die: for the anointing oil of the LORD is upon you. And they did according to the word of Moses [Lev. 10:6–7].

A restriction is placed on Aaron and his two remaining sons. They were not to mourn outwardly. There is a twofold reason for this. The first is clearly stated, "the anointing oil of the LORD is upon you." They were set aside to represent the people before God, and they were God's representatives before the people. They were to continue in their office that there might be a mediator between God and man, lest wrath should come upon the people and the judgment of death be upon them. In the second place, they were not to show the outward signs of mourning which would contradict the action of God in judging their loved ones. It must be added that they must have gone about their office with sad hearts. They were serving God and there must be no evidence of rebellion against Him.

And the LORD spake unto Aaron, saying,

Do not drink wine nor strong drink, thou, nor thy sons with thee, when ye go into the tabernacle of the congregation, lest ye die: it shall be a statute for ever throughout your generations [Lev. 10:8–9].

It would appear from this instruction that Nadab and Abihu had acted under the influence of alcohol. This is one of the finest examples in Scripture against the use and abuse of alcohol or drugs. The priest is to serve the Lord with a clear, steady, and sober mind. Today we have the advocates of the use of drugs in religion. My friend, God despises such an approach to Him. This is the same thing that Paul meant when he said, "And be not drunk with wine, wherein is excess; but be filled with the Spirit" (Eph. 5:18). The believer is to draw his dynamic and his zeal from the Spirit of the Lord and not from frail and human props. What a lesson this is against drugs and alcohol for us today.

> **And that ye may put difference between holy and unholy, and between unclean and clean;**
>
> **And that ye may teach the children of Israel all the statutes which the Lord hath spoken unto them by the hand of Moses [Lev. 10:10–11].**

The use of wine dulls the senses so that a sharp distinction cannot be made between the holy and the unholy. True values are distorted and there is a breakdown in morals as a result of the use and abuse of alcohol. The priest must keep the statutes of the Lord so that he can teach them to the people. It is the filling of the Holy Spirit that is needed for the study and the teaching of the Word of God.

INJUNCTIONS CONCERNING THE OFFERINGS

> **And Moses spake unto Aaron, and unto Eleazar and unto Ithamar, his sons that were left, Take the meat offering that remaineth of the offerings of the Lord made by fire, and eat it without leaven beside the altar: for it is most holy:**
>
> **And ye shall eat it in the holy place, because it is thy due, and thy sons' due, of the sacrifices of the Lord made by fire: for so I am commanded.**

> And the wave breast and heave shoulder shall ye eat in a clean place; thou, and thy sons, and thy daughters with thee: for they be thy due, and thy sons' due, which are given out of the sacrifices of peace offerings of the children of Israel.
>
> The heave shoulder and the wave breast shall they bring with the offerings made by fire of the fat, to wave it for a wave offering before the LORD; and it shall be thine, and thy sons' with thee, by a statute for ever; as the LORD hath commanded [Lev. 10:12–15].

Moses repeats the commandments which concern both the meal offering and the peace offering. A portion of the offering was to be eaten by them in the holy place. This evidently is the outer court beside the burnt altar. It is holy because it was set aside for the service of God. The wave breast and the heave shoulder should be eaten in a clean place. Apparently they could take this to eat in their homes which would be ceremonially clean.

> And Moses diligently sought the goat of the sin offering, and, behold, it was burnt: and he was angry with Eleazar and Ithamar, the sons of Aaron which were left alive, saying,
>
> Wherefore have ye not eaten the sin offering in the holy place, seeing it is most holy, and God hath given it you to bear the iniquity of the congregation, to make atonement for them before the LORD?
>
> Behold, the blood of it was not brought in within the holy place: ye should indeed have eaten it in the holy place, as I commanded [Lev. 10:16–18].

Now here is another tragic incident with action contrary to the will of God. We find failure on the part of the two other sons of Aaron, but here it is a sin of omission. It was not a deliberate and willful sin, as was that of the two dead sons. The sin offering was to be eaten in the holy place and that had not been done. Although the blood had been offered, the portion that belonged to the priests had not been eaten. They had omitted doing this, possibly not realizing the importance of it.

And Aaron said unto Moses, Behold, this day have they offered their sin offering and their burnt offering before the LORD; and such things have befallen me: and if I had eaten the sin offering to day, should it have been accepted in the sight of the LORD?

And when Moses heard that, he was content [Lev. 10:19–20].

Aaron assumed responsibility for his sons. Apparently the tragic incident had caused not only a loss of appetite but also a feeling of unworthiness in continuing to serve before God. Moses was satisfied with the explanation. I think at this point old Aaron felt like resigning.

There is tremendous truth for us to draw from this incident. These men came to God on their own. They were willful and this was blasphemy. God judged them. People today ask me whether it is wrong for them to belong to a church which denies the deity of Christ. Friends, do you think anyone can come to God in such a place, apart from God's will and God's terms? If God struck today as He struck Nadab and Abihu, I think half the church members would be dead. The liberals would be struck for denying the deity of Christ and the forgiveness of His sacrifice for us. Many fundamental church members would be struck down like Ananias and Sapphira for their hypocrisy, their lying to the Holy Spirit. God is dealing in mercy today, giving time for repentance and for men to come to the knowledge of the truth. Otherwise many people would be struck dead.

There is a wonderful lesson for you and for me. When we come to God, we must come on His terms. This is not an arrangement which we can make. We are not making the rules. God is the One who saves and He is the One who says how we shall be saved. Jesus Christ says that no man comes to the Father but by Him.

CHAPTER 11

THEME: The food of God's people—clean and unclean animals; contact with carcasses of unclean animals; contact with carcasses of clean animals; contamination of creeping creatures; classification of clean and unclean made by a holy God

This is a most unusual chapter. We have come now to a radical bifurcation in this book. The subject matter is changed from the priests to the people; from offerings to God to food for man; from worship before God to the walk in this world. The change is made from the sacred to the secular without any change of pace or level. There is no thought that this is anything different.

Today we make a false distinction between the sacred and the secular. We think if it is in the church it is sacred. Even gossip in the church seems to be regarded as sacred (especially if it is couched as a prayer request!). If gossip is outside the church, then it is secular. Friend, all and any of our work can be done to the glory of God. Someone has said,

> I want to dig a ditch so straight and true
> That God can look it through.

Friends, you cannot make a distinction between the sacred and the secular. God moves right out here from that which we would call sacred to that which we would call secular, and He makes no distinction.

This chapter is so unusual because God gives a diet, a menu, for the children of Israel to follow. They are to eat certain things and they are not to eat the things which God keeps off the menu. So here is the important question: Could the God of this vast universe be interested in what His creatures have for dinner? Could the One who orders all of creation prepare a menu for man? This chapter gives the answer: God was and is interested in the details of the lives of His people. No detail is too minute to escape His interest and His concern.

A lady asked G. Campbell Morgan whether he thought we ought to pray to God about the little things in our lives. His answer was, "Madam, can you mention anything in your life that is big to God?" You see, we tend to divide things in our lives as big problems and little problems. They are not divided that way before God. They are all little problems to Him. Yet nothing is too small for His attention and care. There are so many injunctions to us to pray about everything, to worry about nothing.

There are great spiritual lessons for us in this section, as we shall see; but there is also a very real and practical aspect which, because it pertained to Israel, we sometimes ignore. Since God forbade the eating of certain animals and permitted the eating of others, it must be assumed that there was a health factor involved. They could eat certain animals, fish, and birds, but not others. It was not a superstition and it was more than a religious rite to make a distinction between clean and unclean animals. Since God prescribed certain animals for the diet of His people, and since He definitely forbade others, there must be some benefit in following that diet. History should demonstrate that God had good and sufficient grounds for making His distinctions. Now it is true that God could have acted in an arbitrary fashion in setting up these lines of separation between clean and unclean, but, ordinarily, God acted for the good of His people. Does history show this to be the case in these matters?

Well, the interesting thing we will find is that the animals which were forbidden to be eaten were largely unclean feeders. The animals rejected by the Mosaic system are more liable to disease.

Let me give a quotation from Dr. S. H. Kellogg: "One of the greatest discoveries of modern science is the fact that a large number of diseases to which animals are liable are due to the presence of low forms of parasitic life. To such diseases those which are unclean in their feeding will be especially exposed, while none will perhaps be found wholly exempt. Another discovery of recent times which has a no less important bearing on the question raised by this chapter is the now ascertained fact that many of these parasitic diseases are common to both animals and men, and may be communicated from the former to the latter" (*The Book of Leviticus*, p. 314).

He goes on to list the parasite trichinae in swine, diphtheria in turkeys, and glanders in horses. Evidently Moses didn't understand about these diseases and certainly the physicians in Egypt didn't know about them. But God knew! God made these distinctions between clean and unclean. Does this work out in history? It certainly does.

Listen to the statement of Dr. Noel de Mussy, presented to the Paris Academy of Medicine in 1885: "The idea of parasitic and infectious maladies, which has conquered so great a position in modern pathology, appears to have greatly occupied the mind of Moses and to have dominated all his hygienic rules. He excluded from Hebrew dietary *animals particularly liable to parasites*; and as it is in the blood that the germs and spores of infectious disease circulate, he orders that they must be drained of their blood before serving for food."

How did Moses know that? Well, Moses wouldn't have known it, but God told him.

I quote Dr. Kellogg again. "Even so long ago as the days when the plague was desolating Europe, the Jews so universally escaped infection that, by this their exemption, the popular suspicion was excited into fury, and they were accused of causing the fearful mortality among their gentile neighbors by poisoning the wells and springs."

Professor Hosmer wrote: "Throughout the entire history of Israel, the wisdom of the ancient lawgivers in these respects has been remarkably shown. In times of pestilence the Jews have suffered far less than others; as regards longevity and general health, they have in every age been noteworthy, and, at the present day, in the life-insurance offices, the life of a Jew is said to be worth much more than that of men of other stock."

Dr. Behrends also states: "In Prussia, the mean duration of Jewish life averages five years more than that of the general population." Now, of course, today the Jews are breaking down their rules about diet, and the gap is closing. There were times when the life of the Jews was actually twice that of their gentile neighbors.

There are some lessons in this for us today. We are apt to condemn Israel for placing such a great emphasis on the physical while missing the spiritual implications. At the same time, we tend to place such an emphasis on the spiritual that we ignore the physical altogether. A Christian should not ignore his body as to the food he eats, the use and abuse of the body, and the care of it. He should keep in mind that the body is the tabernacle of God today and the very temple of the Holy Spirit. Because a thing is physical does not preclude it from being spiritual.

At the same time, we are told very definitely today, that we can eat whatever we wish to eat. If you want to eat rattlesnake meat, you may eat rattlesnake meat. There is no spiritual value in eating or not eating certain foods. In fact, it is a superstition when you approach it like that. Let us look at several Scriptures concerning this:

"I know, and am persuaded by the Lord Jesus, that there is nothing unclean of itself: but to him that esteemeth any thing to be unclean, to him it is unclean" (Rom. 14:14).

"But meat commendeth us not to God: for neither, if we eat, are we the better; neither, if we eat not, are we the worse" (1 Cor. 8:8).

"Meats for the belly, and the belly for meats: but God shall destroy both it and them . . ." (1 Cor. 6:13).

"Whether therefore ye eat, or drink, or whatsoever ye do, do all to the glory of God" (1 Cor. 10:31).

We should point out that gluttony is strictly forbidden and temperance, or self-control, is a command for a believer under grace.

CLEAN AND UNCLEAN ANIMALS (ON THE LAND)

And the LORD spake unto Moses and to Aaron, saying unto them,

Speak unto the children of Israel, saying, These are the beasts which ye shall eat among all the beasts that are on the earth [Lev. 11:1-2].

God draws a strict line of demarcation between light and darkness, night and day, black and white, right and wrong, clean and unclean. And by the way, God is the One who makes the difference between light and darkness. It is His intent to sharpen man's discriminating nature so that he is sensitive to these God-made distinctions. God wants man to love the good and to loathe the evil. This present age is witnessing the dulling of man's sensibilities to the sharp distinctions between right and wrong and good and bad. Man tries to put everything in life in the gray zone of amorality. God draws these distinctions to drive man to the altar and the shed blood of Christ for cleansing and for forgiveness.

God makes the rules. Someone asks, "How do you know what is right?" The answer is that right is what God says is right! This is His universe. Do you know any better rules than the ones He has made? He's made the rules of the physical realm. (Do you want to defy the law of gravity and jump off the earth? It's an expensive trip, and it will cost you millions of dollars to do it. It put our government in debt to do it, and it will put you in debt to do it.)

God moves into the realm of the everyday life and nothing comes closer to that than what man eats. God declares certain things to be clean and certain to be unclean. Man is to be reminded that he lives in a world where sin abounds. Man must learn to choose the good and shun the evil.

The distinction was moral, yet the clean creatures were wholesome and gave nourishment to the body. The distinction of the clean and unclean animals is older than the Mosaic economy, and we know that Noah recognized such a division.

It is noticeable that the choice of edible animals, fish, and fowl follow generally the pattern of civilized man down through the centuries to the present day. That is no accident. God made the distinction and there are certain animals you want and some you don't want to eat. Another feature we should note is that certain animals were probably healthful in that land and in that day which might not be true elsewhere. Today we have no command concerning clean and unclean animals for food.

There are great moral issues involved in this chapter. Man lives in a world of sin, and God requires recognition of this fact. Choices must be made. Fallen man outside of Eden still has a "tree" of which God says he must not eat. I think the moral objective is primary. You remember that when Peter saw the sheet come down with all kinds of animals and birds in it, he didn't want to eat when God told him to eat. God then told him, "Don't you call unclean what God has called clean" (see Acts 10:11–15). In other words, God makes the rules, and man must make his decisions according to God's rules. This is a tremendous moral lesson.

> **Whatsoever parteth the hoof, and is clovenfooted, and cheweth the cud, among the beasts, that shall ye eat [Lev. 11:3].**

This was the rule to be followed to determine the animals to be eaten. This was repeated in Deuteronomy 14:6, and in that chapter it lists the ox, the sheep, the goat, the hart, the roebuck, the fallow deer, the wild goat, the pygarg, the wild ox, and the chamois.

In Leviticus, the principle and rule are given with a few examples of those which are unclean. In Deuteronomy, the principle and rule are not emphasized, but a more extended list of the clean animals is given. Leviticus emphasizes the negative; Deuteronomy emphasizes the positive.

In Leviticus the division of clean and unclean is sharply drawn although this is not a new commandment. The distinction does not follow any biological division, but a health factor was involved.

Some heathen nations, Persia for example, attributed the creation of certain animals to the good god while other animals were the product of a bad god. God created all the animals. Neither did the nature of the animal, as representing some sin or virtue, make the distinction. For example, the lion was unclean, but it represents the Lord Jesus Christ and is the symbol of the tribe of Judah. That is why Christ is called the Lion of the tribe of Judah.

There is not some mysterious connection between the soul and the body as one finds in some heathen cults today. The nature of the animal is not transferred to the one who eats it. That's just nonsense and superstition. Some vegetarians think people become cruel because they eat animal meat. Well, I've seen some pretty mean folk who are vegetarians. May I say, such ideas are nonsense.

For Israel, the distinction between the clean and unclean animals was part of God's plan to keep them separate from all nations. Even today *Kosher* has a particular meaning to everyone. They were constantly reminded that they lived in a world where choices had to be made.

For the Christian there are some spiritual applications. We have already shown that there is no merit in following a ritual regarding meat. But it is interesting to note that "to meditate" is a figurative expression of a cow chewing the cud. "But his delight is in the law of the LORD; and in his law doth he meditate day and night" (Ps. 1:2). Meditating is a valid application for the chewing of the cud for the spiritual benefit of believers. Likewise, the parting of the hoof speaks of the walk of the believer in separation. "I therefore, the prisoner of the LORD, beseech you that ye walk worthy of the vocation wherewith ye are called" (Eph. 4:1). "And walk in love, as Christ also hath loved us. . . . See then that ye walk circumspectly, not as fools, but as wise" (Eph. 5:2, 15). The relationship between the study of the Word of God and the walk of the believer is intimately tied together. "But continue thou in the things which thou hast learned and hast been assured of, knowing of whom thou has learned them; and that from a child thou hast known the holy scriptures, which are able to make thee wise unto salvation through faith which is in Christ Jesus" (2 Tim. 3:14–15). "But be ye doers of the word, and not hearers only, deceiving your own selves" (James 1:22). My friend, the walk of the believer is tied up with the Word of God. If you are going through this world, you will have to chew the cud, the Word of God, and you will need to have that separated walk that only the Word can produce. The Bible-studying believer, who puts into practice the teaching of the Word of God, identifies himself as a child of God by his work and his walk.

Friend, what kind of tracks are you making? I remember the story

of a man years ago when someone tried to hand him a tract. He asked
what it was and was told it was a tract. He handed it back and said he
couldn't read it. He said, "I'll just watch your tracks."

**Nevertheless these shall ye not eat of them that chew the
cud, or of them that divide the hoof: as the camel, because he cheweth the cud, but divideth not the hoof; he
is unclean unto you.**

**And the coney, because he cheweth the cud, but divideth
not the hoof, he is unclean unto you.**

**And the hare, because he cheweth the cud, but divideth
not the hoof; he is unclean unto you.**

**and the swine, though he divide the hoof, and be cloven-
footed, yet he cheweth not the cud; he is unclean to you.**

**Of their flesh shall ye not eat, and their carcase shall ye
not touch; they are unclean to you [Lev. 11:4–8].**

This is an extended list of animals which are unclean. Evidently,
there must have been some question about these animals. Only
vegetable-eating animals chew the cud. This eliminated the carnivorous animals.

God warned about eating a camel. The reaction would be, "Who
would want to?" Don't you think this adds a note of humor to the
words of our Lord when He accused the Pharisees of straining at a
gnat and swallowing a camel? The camel wasn't only lumpy; he was
unclean. A coney is something like a rabbit and lives in rocky places.
This corresponds to our rabbit. It is quite interesting to me that today
there are those who emphasize that one should not eat pork but I have
never heard them mention that one should not eat rabbit. The swine
divides the hoof but does not chew the cud. The pig seems to be constantly eating but does not chew the cud. It is interesting to note that
pork is still a difficult meat to digest. Swine are unclean animals.
They are unclean in their eating habits.

The Israelite was even forbidden to have contact with the dead carcasses of these unclean animals. The spiritual implications of this are unavoidable.

CLEAN AND UNCLEAN CREATURES (ON THE WATER)

These shall ye eat of all that are in the waters: whatsoever hath fins and scales in the waters, in the seas, and in the rivers, them shall ye eat.

And all that have not fins and scales in the seas, and in the rivers, of all that move in the waters, and of any living thing which is in the waters, they shall be an abomination unto you:

They shall be even an abomination unto you; ye shall not eat of their flesh, but ye shall have their carcases in abomination.

Whatsoever hath no fins nor scales in the waters, that shall be an abomination unto you [Lev. 11:9-12].

There is a sharp line drawn here as well as among animals. The clean fish must be characterized by two visible marks—fins and scales—to be clean. This rule applied to both fresh and saltwater fish. Crawling creatures in the water were forbidden, which would eliminate a great segment of the creatures of the waters. No examples are given, probably because the distinction is very clear cut.

Israel depended on the supply of fish from the Mediterranean Sea, the Sea of Galilee, and the Jordan River. Fish played a prominent part in the diet of the nation. One of the gates of Jerusalem was called the fish gate. This is where the fish from the Mediterranean were brought in, and it is interesting that this was a problem in the times of Nehemiah. The fishermen would bring in their fish on the Sabbath Day (Neh. 13:16–22).

The important role of fishing in the earthly ministry of the Lord Jesus Christ is well known to the student of the New Testament. The first disciples our Lord called were fishermen. They were told that they were to become fishers of men.

Jesus told the parable that the Kingdom of Heaven is like a net which caught good fish and bad fish (Matt. 13:47–50). What was the method of determining the good from the bad fish? It is not whether the fish were large or small but would be according to the Levitical law. A fish that has both fins and scales is clean, or good. Now how is this like the judgment of the wicked from among the just? Well, the believer is the one who is propelled by the Holy Spirit and who is clothed in the righteousness of Christ. Those are the two identifying marks. Those are the fins and the scales, if you please.

CLEAN AND UNCLEAN FLYING CREATURES
(IN THE AIR)

And these are they which ye shall have in abomination among the fowls; they shall not be eaten, they are an abomination: the eagle, and the ossifrage, and the osprey,

And the vulture, and the kite after his kind;

Every raven after his kind;

And the owl, and the night hawk, and the cuckoo, and the hawk after his kind,

And the little owl, and the cormorant, and the great owl,

And the swan, and the pelican, and the gier eagle,

And the stork, the heron after her kind, and the lapwing, and the bat [Lev. 11:13–19].

On the birds there are no visible markers like there are on the fish and the animals. But they seem to have in common that they are all unclean feeders. For the most part, they feed on dead carcasses of animals, fish, and other fowl.

A list of unclean birds of Palestine is given. This is another point that reveals that the Mosaic system was intended for the nation Israel and also for the particular land of Palestine. Some of these birds sound strange to us. They fall into the family of the eagles and the hawks, the vultures and the ravens, the owls and cormorants, and the swans and pelicans. They don't even sound appetizing. They are the "dirty birdies" because of their feeding habits. Now remember, some people eat some of these birds today. I can't say I would like any of them, but whether we eat them or don't eat them makes no difference—meat will not commend us to God. The point is that it was teaching Israel to make a distinction. They had to make a decision about what was clean and unclean.

The lesson for us today is that we must make decisions about our conduct and our profession. We have to make the decision about whether to accept Christ or not, whether to study the Word of God or not, whether to walk in a way pleasing to God or not. That is the application for us today.

This section throws some light on the experience of Elijah. He was fed by the ravens—dirty birds. Elijah did not eat the ravens, but they fed him. This was a humbling experience for this man of God who obeyed God in every detail.

CLEAN AND UNCLEAN CREEPING CREATURES
(ON THE GROUND)

All fowls that creep, going upon all four, shall be an abomination unto you.

Yet these may ye eat of every flying creeping thing that goeth upon all four, which have legs above their feet, to leap withal upon the earth;

Even these of them ye may eat; the locust after his kind, and the bald locust after his kind, and the beetle after his kind, and the grasshopper after his kind.

But all other flying creeping things, which have four feet, shall be an abomination unto you [Lev. 11:20–23].

Well, folks, you can leave all of these off my menu. However, we must note that some of them are clean. There were apparently four species of locusts. The locust was the regular species; the bald locust had a protuberance; the beetle was a locust with a protuberance and a tail; the grasshopper was a locust with a tail but without a protuberance. So they were permitted to eat these four kinds of locusts. But, friend, if you're having me over for dinner, let's have something else on the menu! Although they don't appeal to me, there is nothing religiously or ceremonially unclean about them. John the Baptist had a scriptural diet when he ate locusts and wild honey.

CONTACT WITH CARCASSES OF UNCLEAN ANIMALS

And for these ye shall be unclean: whosoever toucheth the carcase of them shall be unclean until the even.

And whosoever beareth aught of the carcase of them shall wash his clothes, and be unclean until the even.

The carcases of every beast which divideth the hoof, and is not clovenfooted, nor cheweth the cud, are unclean unto you: every one that toucheth them shall be unclean.

And whatsoever goeth upon his paws, among all manner of beasts that go on all four, those are unclean unto you: whoso toucheth their carcase shall be unclean until the even.

And he that beareth the carcase of them shall wash his clothes, and be unclean until the even: they are unclean unto you [Lev. 11:24–28].

Not only was Israel forbidden to eat unclean animals, but also they were forbidden to touch the carcass of an unclean animal. Contamination by contact is the principle here. This was a great principle of life that was restated in the days of the return of Israel after the Captivity. "Thus saith the LORD of hosts; Ask now the priests concerning the law, saying, If one bear holy flesh in the skirt of his garment, and with his skirt do touch bread, or pottage, or wine, or oil, or any meat, shall it be holy? And the priests answered and said, No. Then said Haggai, If one that is unclean by a dead body touch any of these, shall it be unclean? And the priests answered and said, It shall be unclean" (Hag. 2:11–13).

There is a very important principle set before us here. Cleanness or holiness is not transferred by contact. On the contrary, dirt, sin, and unholiness are transferred by contact. In other words, it is impossible to bring holiness out of the unholy. But the unclean can affect the clean. An unrighteous man cannot produce righteous works which are acceptable to God. You cannot bring righteousness out of unrighteousness.

This principle operates as a law in every realm of life and in all strata of society. A gallon of dirty water is not made clean by adding a gallon of clean water. On the other hand, one drop of dirty water will contaminate the clean water. A boy with the measles is never cured by contact with a boy who is well, but the well boy may very well catch the measles from the sick boy. A Christian cannot mingle with the world and play with sin without becoming contaminated. Where do we get the idea that a Christian can dabble with drugs and drinking and night clubs and wild parties? Some claim that the way to reach the lost is to meet them on their level. Well, do they reach the lost that way? No, they are contaminated and take part in those sins themselves. The New Testament is clear on this. "And others save with fear, pulling them out of the fire; hating even the garment spotted by the flesh" (Jude 23). It is a terrible mistake to mix and mingle with sin. We are to beware of all contamination.

An Israelite was reminded of this great principle when he walked along the road and saw a dead dog or a dead bear. He was forbidden to carry the carcass or any part of it. He was not to take a bone or the skin for any use. If he inadvertently touched the carcass of an unclean animal, he was to wash his garments and remain unclean until the end of the day.

These are great spiritual lessons for us. The Christian is sanctified by the redemption of Christ and is clothed with His garments of righteousness. But we walk through the world where we can become contaminated. We still have the old nature. Not until we lay down this body in death will we be completely and totally sanctified and removed from the very presence of sin.

> **These also shall be unclean unto you among the creeping things that creep upon the earth; the weasel, and the mouse, and the tortoise after his kind,**
>
> **And the ferret, and the chameleon, and the lizard, and the snail, and the mole.**
>
> **These are unclean to you among all that creep: whosoever doth touch them, when they be dead, shall be unclean until the even [Lev. 11:29–31].**

These are creatures that live on the ground or under the ground. They must have been rather commonplace but they were to be avoided by the Israelite. The carcass of a mole could contaminate him as much as the carcass of an elephant. So he was constantly reminded that he lived in a world of fallen creatures, and that little sins are as heinous in God's sight as big sins. The mote and the beam are alike to God. "Little sins" are also sin and must be avoided.

> **And upon whatsoever any of them, when they are dead, doth fall, it shall be unclean; whether it be any vessel of wood, or raiment, or skin, or sack, whatsoever vessel it be, wherein any work is done, it must be put into water, and it shall be unclean until the even; so it shall be cleansed.**
>
> **And every earthen vessel, whereinto any of them falleth, whatsoever is in it shall be unclean; and ye shall break it.**

**Of all meat which may be eaten, that on which such wa-
ter cometh shall be unclean: and all drink that may be
drunk in every such vessel shall be unclean.**

**And every thing whereupon any part of their carcase
falleth shall be unclean; whether it be oven, or ranges
for pots, they shall be broken down: for they are unclean, and shall be unclean unto you.**

**Nevertheless a fountain or pit, wherein there is plenty of
water, shall be clean: but that which toucheth their carcase shall be unclean [Lev. 11:32–36].**

Now we go into the kitchen. It must have been a commonplace experience for some rodent to get into the kitchen of that day and fall into
one of the vessels and die. Any earthen vessel had to be broken and
the water or grain or whatever was in it had to be thrown out. A bronze
vessel was to be scoured clean. You see, God taught His people cleanliness in the preparation of food. And he was teaching them a lesson
in holiness. Every vessel was holy to God and it was all to remain
clean. In the Mosaic system, cleanliness was next to godliness and
this applied to even the smallest detail in domestic situations. God
guarded His people against contamination and pollution.

If the dead carcass fell into a fountain or a lake, the water was not
contaminated. It was too big and too fresh.

Isn't it wonderful that the Lord Jesus Christ is the fountain of living
water? He is *not* contaminated by contact with the sinner or the sick,
the leper or the woman with an issue of blood. Jesus said: "But whosoever drinketh of the water that I shall give him shall never thirst; but
the water that I shall give him shall be in him a well of water springing
up into everlasting life" (John 4:14). Also "In the last day, that great
day of the feast, Jesus stood and cried, saying, If any man thirst, let
him come unto me, and drink. He that believeth on me, as the scripture hath said, out of his belly shall flow rivers of living water" (John
7:37–38).

> And if any part of their carcase fall upon any sowing seed which is to be sown, it shall be clean.
>
> But if any water be put upon the seed, and any part of their carcase fall thereon, it shall be unclean unto you [Lev. 11:37–38].

Now we leave the kitchen and go out into the field and the food production. Dry seed that was to be sown could not be contaminated by contact with a carcass of the unclean. However, if the seed was wet, then its shell or armor had been penetrated and it was unclean.

This is why the child of God needs a shell or armor today. We are told, "Put on the whole armour of God, that ye may be able to stand against the wiles of the devil" (Eph. 6:11).

CONTACT WITH CARCASSES OF CLEAN ANIMALS

> And if any beast, of which ye may eat, die; he that toucheth the carcase thereof shall be unclean until the even.
>
> And he that eateth of the carcase of it shall wash his clothes, and be unclean until the even: he also that beareth the carcase of it shall wash his clothes, and be unclean until the even [Lev. 11:39–40].

Any clean animal that died of itself or of disease was unclean. In Malachi 1:8 God forbade the sacrifice of any animal that was lame or sick. God will not accept the second-best or the castoff from us either.

CONTAMINATION OF CREEPING CREATURES

> And every creeping thing that creepeth upon the earth shall be an abomination; it shall not be eaten.
>
> Whatsoever goeth upon the belly, and whatsoever goeth upon all four, or whatsoever hath more feet among all

> creeping things that creep upon the earth, them ye shall not eat; for they are an abomination.
>
> Ye shall not make yourselves abominable with any creeping thing that creepeth, neither shall ye make yourselves unclean with them, that ye should be defiled thereby [Lev. 11:41–43].

Everything that crept on the earth or that went on its belly was unclean. God gives the reason they should not become unclean with them:

> For I am the LORD your God: ye shall therefore sanctify yourselves, and ye shall be holy; for I am holy: neither shall ye defile yourselves with any manner of creeping thing that creepeth upon the earth.
>
> For I am the LORD that bringeth you up out of the land of Egypt, to be your God: ye shall therefore be holy, for I am holy [Lev. 11:44–45].

All creeping things were unclean as representatives of the fall of man when the serpent was cursed and made to crawl on its belly.

CLASSIFICATION OF CLEAN AND UNCLEAN MADE BY A HOLY GOD

> This is the law of the beasts, and of the fowl, and of every living creature that moveth in the waters, and of every creature that creepeth upon the earth:
>
> To make a difference between the unclean and the clean, and between the beast that may be eaten and the beast that may not be eaten [Lev. 11:46–47].

It is God who makes the sharp distinction between the clean and the unclean. Holiness in little things is essential. This is the real test of

God's man. The acid test of any life of any of God's people is this. God says, "I am your Lord. I am holy. Be ye holy."

My friend, you must make the decision as to whether you are going to walk with God and for God in this contaminated world. This is the lesson for us from this chapter of the clean and the unclean.

CHAPTER 12

Theme: Cleansing of a mother after childbirth; a sacrifice for atonement

In the preceding chapter we saw the contamination of sin by contact. The external character of sin was emphasized—we live in a world surrounded by sin.

This chapter places the emphasis on the internal character of sin. Not only do we become sinners by contact, but we are sinners by birth. And this chapter is the law concerning motherhood, the transmission of sin by inheritance. The very nature that we inherit is a fallen, sinful nature. David said, "Behold, I was shapen in iniquity, and in sin did my mother conceive me" (Ps. 51:5). This chapter is in the field of obstetrics, as the former chapter was in the field of dietetics and pediatrics. Our Lord is the Great Physician and He is the specialist in all fields.

Pagan people entertained superstitious notions about the uncleanness of women in childbirth. There is not a shred of that notion in the Levitical economy, as we hope to point out. It was also a pagan practice to place women in an inferior position to man. This law does not contain a breath of that idea, as the Mosaic economy lifted womanhood and ennobled motherhood in contrast to the base heathenism that surrounded the nation Israel.

Obviously there were certain hygienic benefts in the practice of these God-given laws—as we saw in the matter of diet. God was caring for His people physically, and at the same time was teaching them (and us) the great spiritual truth that we are born in sin.

There is a doctrine today that is almost totally rejected, and that is the total depravity of man—but man is certainly *demonstrating* it! Our news media is full of it, and man's total depravity is quite obvious. We are told: "Wherefore, as by one man sin entered into the world, and death by sin; and so death passed upon all men, for that all have sinned" (Rom. 5:12).

The world thinks of innocence, virtue, and goodness in the picture of a young mother holding a sweet, cuddly baby in her arms. But God paints a different picture, an opposite portrait, in this chapter. There's the young mother holding the precious baby, but he's not a picture of innocence and sinlessness. He is a picture of uncleanness and sin. Do you know what happened? That mother brought into the world a sinner. That's all she could bring into the world because she is a sinner—and Papa's a sinner too.

S. H. Kellogg has this comment: "In the birth of a child, the special original curse against the woman is regarded by the law as reaching its fullest, most consummate and significant expression. For the extreme evil of the state of sin into which the first woman, by that first sin, brought all womanhood, is seen most of all in this, that now woman, by means of those powers given her for good and blessing, can bring into the world only a child of sin" (*The Book of Leviticus*, p. 314).

You recall that God said to the first woman: ". . . I will greatly multiply thy sorrow and thy conception; in sorrow thou shalt bring forth children; and thy desire shall be to thy husband, and he shall rule over thee" (Gen. 3:16). Not only would the woman travail in bringing a child into the world, but the chances are that child would be a heartbreak to her because that child is a sinner.

That is, I think, what Paul had in mind when he put down certain regulations concerning woman's place in public worship. He says: "But I suffer not a woman to teach, nor to usurp authority over the man, but to be in silence" (1 Tim. 2:12). He is talking about the place of doctrinal leadership in the church, and I think the reason is twofold. Adam was created first, and also in the transgression the woman was the one who was deceived. "For Adam was first formed, then Eve. And Adam was not deceived, but the woman being deceived was in the transgression" (1 Tim. 2:13–14). This is not teaching the superiority of man over woman. Rather, it is a matter of order and headship. Secondly, the woman was first in the transgression—she was the leader there.

The fact that a Christian mother travails in the birth of her child is an evidence of God's judgment, but it certainly does not mean she loses her salvation when she brings a sinner into the world. "Notwithstanding she shall be saved in childbearing, if they continue in faith and charity and holiness with sobriety" (1 Tim. 2:15). She is not saved *by* childbearing; she is saved *through* childbearing. In other words, she does not become unclean and lose her salvation by bringing a sinner into the world. The evidence of her salvation is in her faith, love, holy living, and sobriety. "Uncleanness" under the Law reminded her that she had brought a sinner into the world. "Travail" under grace reminds the mother today that a sinner has been born even though she is a believer.

When Paul the apostle said to the Philippian jailer, "Believe on the Lord Jesus Christ, and thou shalt be saved, and thy house" (Acts 16:31) he didn't mean that his family would be saved just because he believed on the Lord. Neither does it mean that your children are saved just because you are a believer. Discipline has broken down in the homes of America because too many parents think they are raising a sweet little flower when what they have is a stinkweed! That, my friend, is what you and I are, and that is what we have brought into the world. Again and again I asked my daughter, "Are you sure you trust Christ? Are you saved?" She asked me once, "Why do you keep asking me?" And I told her, "I just want to make sure." She has my nature and I happen to know that this nature of mine is a lost nature. She is not automatically saved just because I am a Christian and a preacher of the gospel.

This raises another question. Someone said, "If my baby is born a sinner and he dies in infancy, is he lost because he is a sinner?" No. In Adam all die, and that's the reason the little one died. But the Lord Jesus said, "Take heed that ye despise not one of these little ones; for I say unto you, That in heaven their angels [spirits] do always behold the face of my Father which is in heaven" (Matt. 18:10). The word "angels" should be translated *spirits*—their spirits behold the face of the Father. In other words, when that little infant dies, his spirit goes to be with the Father. Why? Because Christ came down and died for sinners, and the little one has not reached the age of accountability. The minute he does, then he has to make a decision for Christ.

I like the quaint epitaph that Robert Robertson placed over the graves of his four children:

Bold infidelity, turn pale and die,
Beneath this stone four infants' ashes lie;
Say are they lost or saved,
If death's by sin, they sinned for they lie here;
If Heaven's by works, in Heaven they can't appear.
Reason—Ah, how depraved.
Reverse the Bible's sacred page, the knot's untied.
They died, for Adam sinned; they live, for Jesus died.

CLEANSING OF A MOTHER AT THE BIRTH OF A MALE CHILD

And the Lord spake unto Moses, saying,

Speak unto the children of Israel, saying, If a woman have conceived seed, and born a man child: then she shall be unclean seven days; according to the days of the separation for her infirmity shall she be unclean [Lev. 12:1–2].

The mother is unclean because she has brought a sinner into the world. Eve thought she had brought the Savior into the world when Cain was born, but she had brought into the world only a sinner—the first murderer. Now this Levitical ritual is to remind women that they were bringing into the world the same kind of a baby that Eve had brought into the world. They cannot do good. They can only sin.

Her uncleanness is divided into two periods. The first period was seven days. We shall see in the next verse that the male child was circumcised on the eighth day. Circumcision was the badge given to Abraham.

I realize that the idea of uncleanness of motherhood conflicts with the popular notion of motherhood and the little baby, but we need to emphasize that the babies we are bringing into the world are sinners.

They are going to run undisciplined. They will be revolutionaries. They will adopt the new morality, which is just old-fashioned sin. The whole philosophy of life has been entirely wrong. We need to start raising children by the Scripture and not by Dr. Spock. This has been the cause of deep problems during my entire time in the ministry—I have seen parents after parents raise their children in this way.

And in the eighth day the flesh of his foreskin shall be circumcised.

And she shall then continue in the blood of her purifying three and thirty days; she shall touch no hallowed thing, nor come into the sanctuary, until the days of her purifying be fulfilled [Lev. 12:3-4].

We have mentioned that the mother's period of uncleanness is divided into two periods. The first was seven days, and then the male child was circumcised on the eighth day. Being born an Israelite did not include him in the covenant until the baby was circumcised. Each Israelite was first of all a son of Adam and was born outside the covenant. This is what Paul means in Romans 9:6-7: ". . . For they are not all Israel, which are of Israel: neither, because they are the seed of Abraham, are they all children . . ." Natural birth does not bring a man into a right relationship with God. Natural birth separates a man from God! God owes us nothing. He sent His Son out of His grace to us.

The second period of the mother's uncleanness was for thirty-three days so that the total time was forty days. This reaffirms the fact that the rite of circumcision had a meaning of cleansing. It was God's way in the Old Testament of saying, ". . . Suffer little children, and forbid them not to come unto me . . ." (Matt. 19:14). The circumcision of the male child removed some of the sin from the mother. His acceptance meant her acceptance also. She is reminded that she is still a sinner, and thirty-three more days are required for her cleansing.

It is interesting to note that Jesus was circumcised on the eighth day. Then Jesus was brought to the temple when the days of Mary's purification according to the Law of Moses were accomplished (Luke 2:21-23). Mary was a sinner even though she brought the sinless Savior into the world. His birth did not save her. Only her new birth by accepting Jesus as her own Savior could save her.

Jesus was circumcised to fulfill the Law of Moses. He came to fulfill, not to destroy the Law. He was made (born) under the Law. Thus he identified Himself perfectly with His people.

CLEANSING OF THE MOTHER AT THE BIRTH OF A FEMALE CHILD

But if she bear a maid child, then she shall be unclean two weeks, as in her separation: and she shall continue in the blood of her purifying threescore and six days [Lev. 12:5].

The time is doubled for the cleansing at the birth of a female child. I don't know why this was so, but obviously the circumcision of the male child had something to do with the reduction of the days and it relieved some of the curse.

Grace brings us to a new day. "For as many of you as have been baptized into Christ have put on Christ. There is neither Jew nor Greek, there is neither bond nor free, there is neither male nor female: for ye are all one in Christ Jesus. And if ye be Christ's, then are ye Abraham's seed, and heirs according to the promise" (Gal. 3:27–29).

CLEANSING OF THE MOTHER BY BRINGING A SACRIFICE FOR ATONEMENT

And when the days of her purifying are fulfilled, for a son, or for a daughter, she shall bring a lamb of the first year for a burnt offering, and a young pigeon, or a turtledove, for a sin offering, unto the door of the tabernacle of the congregation, unto the priest:

Who shall offer it before the LORD, and make an atonement for her; and she shall be cleansed from the issue of

her blood. This is the law for her that hath born a male or a female.

And if she be not able to bring a lamb, then she shall bring two turtles, or two young pigeons; the one for the burnt offering, and the other for a sin offering: and the priest shall make an atonement for her, and she shall be clean [Lev. 12:6–8].

The mother brought a burnt offering and a sin offering to God and the priest offered it for her. She certainly was not saved just by bringing children into the world, as some claim. She had to have a sacrifice. A mother must trust the Lord Jesus Christ. With that in mind, she is prepared to raise her child as a sinner who needs to accept Christ. Oh, how the home needs that today!

You remember that when the Lord Jesus was born, his mother brought turtledoves because the poor could bring them as an offering. She had to have an offering because she was a sinner; she was not sinless. She brought an offering. But there was no offering for the Lord Jesus. No offering was ever made for Jesus or by Jesus. He is the sinless One. He was the offering for the sin of the world. He is the Lamb of God.

Friends, think on these things. We live in a world that has gone crazy, has gone mad. This world has turned its back upon the Almighty God, and the judgment of God is beginning to fall upon the world. We are demonstrating the fact that only sinners are born into this world and that all people need the saving grace of God. All people need the shed blood of Christ to pay the penalty for their sins.

CHAPTER 13

THEME: *Diagnosis of leprosy; disposal of lepers' garments*

This is concerned with the exceeding sinfulness of sin. "For out of the heart proceed evil thoughts, murders, adulteries, fornications, thefts, false witness, blasphemies: these are the things which defile a man: but to eat with unwashen hands defileth not a man" (Matt. 15:19–20).

We come now to another unusual section of this book, the section on leprosy. Someone may ask whether this is practical for today. May I say that all of this book is practical. We are in the section of the book which we have entitled "Holiness in Daily Life." God is concerned with the conduct of His children. We saw that He is concerned with their food; now in chapters 13, 14, and 15 we find He is concerned with leprosy and the cleansing of running issues.

Leprosy and running issues of the flesh are accurate symbols of the manifestation of sin in the heart of man. It shows the exceeding sinfulness of sin and the effect of sin in action. The emphasis of Leviticus is on sin.

In the heart of this book on worship of a holy God is this extended section on leprosy and issues in the flesh. The filthiness and repulsiveness of sin are represented in leprosy. The hopelessness and deadliness of sin are accurately portrayed. The leper who trudged down a hot, dusty, oriental road crying out, "Unclean! Unclean!" was a reminder to the Israelite that he, too, was a moral leper who needed supernatural cleansing.

Perhaps you are one of those who thinks that you will be saved by your works and that you don't need Christ as your Savior. May I say that if you could go to heaven just like you are, without Christ, you would go through heaven crying out, "Unclean! Unclean!" No angel would touch you with a twenty-foot pole. You couldn't come anywhere near the presence of God.

You see, man has the idea that he has some kind of claim on God, but we have no claim upon Him whatsoever. He owes us nothing. He could blot out of existence this little earth that we live on, and it would not even make a dent in this universe. But thank God, He loves us. I'm so glad He loves us! That is the only thing that could bind Him to us.

God is driving a point home to us, and it is the same point He was driving home to Israel: Sin is exceeding sinful. This comparison between leprosy and sin is a recurring theme in the Scripture: "There is no soundness in my flesh because of thine anger; neither is there any rest in my bones because of my sin. . . . My wounds stink and are corrupt because of my foolishness. . . . For my loins are filled with a loathsome disease: and there is no soundness in my flesh. . . . For I will declare mine iniquity; I will be sorry for my sin" (Ps. 38:3, 5, 7, 18). That is the way we look to God.

Isaiah also had leprosy in his thinking as he described the sins of his people: "From the sole of the foot even unto the head there is no soundness in it; but wounds, and bruises, and putrefying sores: they have not been closed, neither bound up, neither mollified with ointment" (Isa. 1:6). "Surely he hath borne our griefs, and carried our sorrows: yet we did esteem him stricken, smitten of God, and afflicted. But he was wounded for our transgressions, he was bruised for our iniquities: the chastisement of our peace was upon him; and with his stripes we are healed" (Isa. 53:4–5). Now, some folk say he is talking about leprosy here and that he is referring to a physical disease. No, my friend, Isaiah is talking about sin being laid on the Lord Jesus Christ. Can we be sure of that? Listen to the apostle Peter: "Who his own self bare our sins in his own body on the tree, that we, being dead to sins, should live unto righteousness: by whose stripes ye were healed" (1 Pet. 2:24).

We were dead in sin and He bare our sins in His own body on the tree. By His stripes we are healed. Now it is true that physical disease is a manifestation of sin and that behind disease germs there lies sin. If there were no sin, there would be neither death nor sickness.

There are two important considerations we should take into account as we get into this chapter.

1. The Bible does not agree with the generally accepted view that leprosy was incurable in that day. Cleansing is mentioned in Leviticus 14:2. There were supernatural cures such as Naaman's in 2 Kings 5. Some expositors think that Job had leprosy. Since there was no scientific diagnosis of the disease in those days, there has been discussion on what the leprosy was. They had medicines in that day which they used for the cure of leprosy.

This chapter and the following do not contain a cure for leprosy. This should be carefully noted. It gives instructions to the priest on how a case of leprosy is to be determined, and the measures to be taken to prevent its spreading in the camp. After it had been cleansed, there was a ritual to be followed. It is not a cure that is presented here. In chapter 14 it deals with the ceremonial cleansing of the leper after his cure and not the cure itself. The main objective was to teach great spiritual truths in connection with the cleansing of leprosy as a type of sin.

2. This is not a scientific treatise on the detection, prevention, and cure of leprosy. There is no attempt to give a medical diagnosis of the disease. The diagnosis was a practical one which was adjusted to the knowledge of that day. It has direct and definite spiritual lessons for this day. The ritual was ceremonial rather than curative.

There has been some discussion on the part of some Christian physicians as to whether leprosy as we know it is the disease that the Mosaic system is considering. There has been much written in the past, both pro and con. It would seem that the descriptions in these chapters describe leprosy as we understand this loathsome and death-dealing disease but includes also elephantiasis, skin diseases, running issues, cancer, tumors, and social diseases. This is illustrated in chapter 15, and we will amplify this aspect when we come to that chapter. After all, only the first stages of leprosy are described here. By the time the person was declared to be a leper, he was ejected from society.

This chapter deals with the cleansing of leprosy, not the cure of leprosy. The leper was cleansed after he had been cured.

DIAGNOSIS OF A NEW CASE OF LEPROSY

And the LORD spake unto Moses and Aaron, saying,

When a man shall have in the skin of his flesh a rising, a scab, or bright spot, and it be in the skin of his flesh like the plague of leprosy; then he shall be brought unto Aaron the priest, or unto one of his sons the priests [Lev. 13:1–2].

Compared to modern techniques of diagnosis, the methods of Leviticus seem very crude. The procedure was adapted to the knowledge of that day. The diagnosis was not done in order to prescribe a treatment, but rather, it was a religious ritual. This needs to be stated emphatically.

Now friends, since I have a cancer, I know how my doctor treated me. He looked at it and just by looking he came to the conclusion that it was a cancer. It was not until a biopsy had been taken in a scientific way that they decided that they should operate. So in that day, they could have known a great deal more than we realize. The priests handled literally thousands of cases, I think, and so they would know what to look for. Perhaps this isn't as crude as we today think that it was. It may have actually been a pretty good diagnostic system. Still, the emphasis here is upon the spiritual ceremony rather than the physical catharsis.

Three symptoms are identified here: a rising or boil, a scab or small tumor, a bright spot. These are symptoms of leprosy, but the person having such a symptom need not necessarily be a leper. The first step was to bring the patient with a symptom to Aaron or one of the priests,

Just so, any manifestation of sin, either small or great, should be brought immediately to our Great High Priest, who is also the Great Physician. We are to pray about everything. That includes every manifestation of sin. That is the place to go when we are physically sick, too. I received a caustic letter not so long ago telling me not to be so proud and go to a certain healer. They said I would be healed if my pride would be overcome. Friends, I took my case to the Great Physician, the Lord Jesus. I go there when I sin, and I go there when I am sick. That is the place to go first. That doesn't mean I didn't go to a doctor when I got sick. But I went to the Lord Jesus first! "Let us therefore come boldly unto the throne of grace, that we may obtain mercy, and find grace to help in time of need. . . . Wherefore he is able also to save them to the uttermost that come unto God by him, seeing he ever liveth to make intercession for them" (Heb. 4:16; 7:25). "If we confess our sins, he is faithful and just to forgive us our sins, and to cleanse us from all unrighteousness" (1 John 1:9).

And the priest shall look on the plague in the skin of the flesh: and when the hair in the plague is turned white, and the plague in sight be deeper than the skin of his flesh, it is a plague of leprosy: and the priest shall look on him, and pronounce him unclean [Lev. 13:3].

There was no rash judgment made. The man or woman was carefully watched over a period of time. If a lesion on the skin began to disappear, the person was dismissed. If the hair turned white, it was becoming dead and showed that the disease was beneath the skin. Then the priest would pronounce the person unclean.

The Great Physician has made a thorough inspection of us and has made a diagnosis. "Their throat is an open sepulchre; with their tongues they have used deceit; the poison of asps is under their lips: whose mouth is full of cursing and bitterness: their feet are swift to shed blood: destruction and misery are in their ways" (Rom. 3:13–16). God says, "All have sinned." We are unclean. You see, just like any doctor, the Great Physician asks us to open our mouth and He looks down our throat. Then He asks us to stick out our tongue and there He finds deceit and lying. We are all spiritual lepers. God cannot have lepers in heaven. He must cure them before they get there.

Leprosy is a type of sin.

1. It becomes overt in loathsome ways. One night a drunken man came in off the street and sat in our warm auditorium. Suddenly he

collapsed and fell out of the seat. We had to call an ambulance. By the time the ambulance got there, he was a mess. May I say to you, sin is loathsome in many ways.

2. It is a horrible disease. Dr. Kellogg wrote, "From among all diseases, leprosy has been selected by the Holy Ghost to stand . . . as the supreme type of sin, as seen by God!"

3. It begins in a small way, "a rising, a scab, a bright spot." Finally it delivers a death-dealing blow. What is at first so very small becomes a frightful and dreadful condition. Lepers in most countries today are isolated from the populace and are segregated into hospitals or colonies. Those of us who have seen pictures of lepers from missionaries in Africa or Asia realize what a dread disease it is. A century ago a missionary, William Thompson, described leprosy in Palestine in *The Land and the Book*: "As I was approaching Jerusalem, I was startled by the sudden apparition of a crowd of beggars, sans eyes, sans nose, sans hair, sans everything. . . . They held up their handless arms, unearthly sounds gurgled through throats without palates; in a word, I was horrified!" (Vol. I, pp. 530–531).

Sin seems ever so infinitesimal in a child. It may appear as a bright spot at first. The parents and relatives think little Willie is cute when he acts up, yells and kicks his feet in the air. Unless Willie is disciplined and is led to a saving knowledge of Christ, he will become lawless and even criminal. Lenin, Stalin, and Hitler were all cute little babies once upon a time.

No drunkard ever became an alcoholic by taking one drink, but no man ever became an alcoholic who did not take the first drink. All sins start small.

4. Leprosy not only progresses slowly from a small beginning, but it progresses surely. From a little beginning, it advances surely and steadily to a tragic crisis. I quote Dr. Thompson again: "It comes on by degrees in different parts of the body: the hair falls from the head and eyebrows; the nails loosen, decay, and drop off; joint after joint of the fingers and toes shrink up and slowly fall away: the gums are absorbed, and the teeth disappear; the nose, the eyes, the tongue, and the palate are slowly consumed; and, finally, the wretched victim sinks into the earth and disappears."

This is the way God says sin is. "Then when lust hath conceived, it bringeth forth sin: and sin, when it is finished, bringeth forth death" (James 1:15).

Leprosy is a living death. A leper was treated as a dead man. The wages of sin is death. "Be not deceived; God is not mocked: for whatsoever a man soweth, that shall he also reap. For he that soweth to his flesh shall of the flesh reap corruption; but he that soweth to the Spirit shall of the Spirit reap life everlasting" (Gal. 6:7–8).

Like leprosy, sin destroys the whole man. Both are corrosive in their effect, working slowly and surely, until finally they break out in an angry display that eventuates in death. No man ever went wrong overnight. Leprosy did not kill in a day—it is not like a heart attack. The leper's life was a walking death. Just so, the sinner is also dead even while he lives. Paul writes, "And you hath he quickened, who were dead in trespasses and sins; wherein in time past ye walked according to the course of this world . . ." (Eph. 2:1–2).

The final, desperate, and inescapable end of sin and leprosy is death.

5. Leprosy does not produce sharp and unbearable pain as some other diseases. Leprosy keeps the man sad and restless. Likewise, sin produces a restlessness and sadness in man that is evident in our culture. Folks want to be amused, want to be made to laugh because they are sad. Crowds flock to places of amusement, to the night clubs, to be entertained. Take a look at the sad faces with vacant stares. Watch the cars filled with restless folk going nowhere fast. We have a generation with itchy feet. It is leprosy.

Finally sin brings a person to the point of not having any feeling, just as Paul said, "Who being past feeling have given themselves over unto lasciviousness, to work all uncleanness with greediness" (Eph. 4:19). They lapse into a state of sad contentment. They can reach the state of having a ". . . conscience seared with a hot iron" (1 Tim. 4:2).

6. Leprosy is thought to be hereditary. Whether it is or not, sin is! All that sinners can bring into the world are more sinners. I am interested in the insight of a contemporary psychologist who recognizes that while the assumption of education is that "the moral nature of man is capable of improvement," the assumption of traditional Chris-

tianity is that "the moral nature of man is corrupt, or absolutely bad."
He further observes that while education assumes that an exterior
"human agent" may be the means of man's "moral improvement," traditional Christianity assumes that "the agent is God" and that rather
than the moral nature of man being improved, "it is exchanged for a
new one."

7. Finally, leprosy and sin separate from God. It seemed cruel that
the leper was not only shut out from society, but also from the sanctuary. It must be remembered that God is holy, the Author of righteousness and cleanliness. Therefore, leprosy is a fitting symbol of sin that
separates from God. "But your iniquities have separated between you
and your God, and your sins have hid his face from you, that he will
not hear" (Isa. 59:2). In the New Jerusalem, the unforgiven and un-
washed sinner is shut out from the presence of God according to Revelation 21:27 and 22:15.

So leprosy stands as a perfect type of sin. It is sin, as it were, made
visible in the flesh. The priest was to look on the leper and pronounce
him unclean. Just so, the Great Physician looks on the human family
and pronounces it unclean. He does this so that we might come to
Him for cleansing. He is ready to touch the leper and make him clean.

I have spent a long time in the beginning of this chapter because it
is so important to see the analogy here and get the great spiritual message for us today. There is not much being said about sin today, yet our
basic problem is sin!

**If the bright spot be white in the skin of his flesh, and in
sight be not deeper than the skin, and the hair thereof be
not turned white; then the priest shall shut up him that
hath the plague seven days [Lev. 13:4].**

Now in this verse we see that there was no haste in making the judgment. Likewise, God is slow to anger in His relationship with us. God
is very patient and He grants every opportunity to the sinner. ". . . The
Lord, The Lord God, merciful and gracious, longsuffering, and abundant in goodness and truth, keeping mercy for thousands, forgiving
iniquity and transgression and sin, and that will by no means clear

the guilty; visiting the iniquity of the fathers upon the children, and upon the children's children, unto the third and to the fourth generation" (Exod. 34:6–7). That verse is in the Old Testament. What does the New Testament say about the patience of God? "The Lord is not slack concerning his promise, as some men count slackness; but is longsuffering to us-ward, not willing that any should perish, but that all should come to repentance" (2 Pet. 3:9).

You see, the priest shut up the man for seven days. He thought it was leprosy, but he was patient with him. Just so, God has shut up the world in quarantine for the disease of sin. "For God hath concluded them all in unbelief, that he might have mercy upon all" (Rom. 11:32). "But the scripture hath concluded all under sin, that the promise by faith of Jesus Christ might be given to them that believe" (Gal. 3:22). "Concluded" means to shut up together. God has the world shut up in quarantine, my friend, and He is not going to let man get very far out into His universe. It is rather amusing that when they brought the men back from the moon, they checked to see if they had brought any disease down here. Do you think we left any disease up there? God has us here under quarantine so that He might have mercy on us.

And the priest shall look on him the seventh day: and, behold, if the plague in his sight be at a stay, and the plague spread not in the skin; then the priest shall shut him up seven days more [Lev. 13:5].

After seven days the priest makes another inspection and if there is still an element of uncertainty, then the patient is placed in quarantine for seven more days. There was not a rash or hasty judgment. We should learn from this that we are not to make hasty and rash judgments of others. It is a serious matter to make a false charge against another believer. Paul told Timothy, "Against an elder receive not an accusation, but before two or three witnesses" (1 Tim. 5:19). He also warned that at the end times there would be false accusers.

When I was a pastor I made a rule that no one could come to me to criticize a church officer unless the accused man was present to hear it. Do you know how many accusations I heard in the last twenty-one years? Just one. We need to be careful.

> **And the priest shall look on him again the seventh day: and behold, if the plague be somewhat dark, and the plague spread not in the skin, the priest shall pronounce him clean: it is but a scab: and he shall wash his clothes, and be clean [Lev. 13:6].**

If the plague in the skin has not spread in fourteen days, but has improved, it obviously was not leprosy and the man is pronounced clean. Those were sweet words for the man, and he surely could sing a jubilee song. He did not need to be separated from his loved ones, but was clean and could go back to them.

Remember that the Lord touched the leper who came to Him and made him clean. More than that, He says to the spiritual lepers that their sins are forgiven. He healed the physical disease to demonstrate that He is the Savior who can forgive sins. Remember how the scribes and the Pharisees asked, ". . . Who can forgive sins, but God alone?" (Luke 5:21). So Jesus first told the man who was paralyzed that his sins were forgiven. Then He said, "But that ye may know that the Son of man hath power upon earth to forgive sins, I say unto thee, Arise, and take up thy couch, and go into thine house." It is important to recognize that Jesus has the authority to do both. (See Luke 5:17–26.)

> **But if the scab spread much abroad in the skin, after that he hath been seen of the priest for his cleansing, he shall be seen of the priest again:**
>
> **And if the priest see that, behold, the scab spreadeth in the skin, then the priest shall pronounce him unclean: it is a leprosy [Lev. 13:7–8].**

This is the dark side of the picture. This would now be the third inspection. Does God give a man a second chance? My friend, God will give the sinner a thousand chances, if that is what it takes.

Finally the verdict must be rendered. The man is declared a leper. It is an awful sentence. The man is put out. Contrast this to the man who was hanging under the sentence of leprosy and was expecting to be put out but then was declared to be clean. That cleansed man did not live like a leper from that day on. He is clean and he lives clean. What a lesson that is for us!

There are some folk who make a profession of being converted. They can stand inspection for a while but finally the awful disease of sin will break out in its frightful symptoms and it is obvious they are unclean. John speaks of this in 1 John 2:19, "They went out from us, but they were not of us; for if they had been of us, they would no doubt have continued with us: but they went out, that they might be made manifest that they were not all of us." Peter describes these unclean and immoral lepers as the dog returning to his own vomit and the sow returning to the mire (2 Pet. 2:22).

DIAGNOSIS OF AN OLD CASE OF LEPROSY

When the plague of leprosy is in a man, then he shall be brought unto the priest;

And the priest shall see him: and, behold, if the rising be white in the skin, and it have turned the hair white, and there be quick raw flesh in the rising;

It is an old leprosy in the skin of his flesh, and the priest shall pronounce him unclean, and shall not shut him up: for he is unclean [Lev. 13:9–11].

This is a case of old leprosy, or we might call it chronic leprosy. There was no need to shut this man up for observation because he was definitely a leper.

There are hardened sinners who are so obviously sinners that even their best friends tell them so. Under this class would come the spiritual Mafia, the murderer and the thief and the alcoholic and the drug addict. These people are under the slavery of their sin and only a supernatural remedy can help in cases like this.

The polished and slick church member who is unsaved does not believe that he has leprosy. He resents being told that he is a lost sinner. The hardened sinner is easier to reach than he, and is more open to the gospel message. He *knows* he has leprosy.

> **And if a leprosy break out abroad in the skin, and the leprosy cover all the skin of him that hath the plague from his head even to his foot . . . Then the priest shall consider . . . he shall pronounce him clean that hath the plague: it is all turned white: he is clean.**
>
> **But when raw flesh appeareth in him, he shall be unclean . . . it is a leprosy. . . .**
>
> **Or if the raw flesh turn again, and be changed unto white . . . then the priest shall pronounce him clean that hath the plague: he is clean [Lev. 13:12–17].**

This section shows another aspect of old leprosy. Although the entire body is covered, it does not necessarily follow that the case is hopeless. The remarkable statement here is that if the flesh has turned white, the patient is declared clean. This seems to indicate clearly that no sinner is hopeless. This may be what Isaiah meant when he wrote: "Why should ye be stricken any more? ye will revolt more and more: the whole head is sick, and the whole heart faint" (Isa. 1:5). Then follows the great invitation of the Great Physician, "Come now, and let us reason together, saith the LORD: though your sins be as scarlet, they shall be as white as snow; though they be red like crimson, they shall be as wool" (Isa. 1:18).

Notice that the true mark and symptom of leprosy is the raw flesh. The Bible has much to say about the flesh, even flesh as it is manifested in the believer: ". . . for all flesh had corrupted his way upon the earth" (Gen. 6:12). ". . . The flesh profiteth nothing . . ." (John 6:63). "For I know that in me, (that is, in my flesh,) dwelleth no good thing . . ." (Rom. 7:18). "That no flesh should glory in his presence . . . flesh and blood cannot inherit the kingdom of God . . ." (1 Cor. 1:29 and 15:50). ". . . Fulfilling the desires of the flesh and of the mind; and were by nature the children of wrath, even as others" (Eph. 2:3). "For we are the circumcision, which worship God in the spirit, and rejoice in Christ Jesus, and have no confidence in the flesh" (Phil. 3:3). "And others save with fear, pulling them out of the fire; hating even the garment spotted by the flesh" (Jude 23).

It is obvious from these passages that the raw flesh is the old nature which was judged on the Cross. When it manifests itself in a believer, God must judge it. The flesh can never please God. Only that which the Holy Spirit produces in the life of the believer is acceptable to God.

DIAGNOSIS OF LEPROSY FROM A BOIL OR A BURN

> The flesh also, in which, even in the skin thereof, was a boil, and is healed,
>
> And in the place of the boil there be a white rising, or a bright spot, white, and somewhat reddish, and it be shewed to the priest;
>
> And if, when the priest seeth it, behold, it be in sight lower than the skin, and the hair thereof be turned white; the priest shall pronounce him unclean: it is a plague of leprosy broken out of the boil.
>
> But if the priest look on it, and, behold, there be no white hairs therein, and if it be not lower than the skin, but be somewhat dark; then the priest shall shut him up seven days:
>
> And if it spread much abroad in the skin, then the priest shall pronounce him unclean: it is a plague.
>
> But if the bright spot stay in his place, and spread not, it is a burning boil; and the priest shall pronounce him clean [Lev. 13:18–23].

These verses give the details of the inspection of a boil. It was to be inspected by the priest because of a possibility of leprosy beginning there. It is just like a small sore which may become cancerous. They followed the same process as in the new case of leprosy. If there were white hair in the boil and it penetrated lower than the skin, these indicated deep-seated trouble. The seven days of inspection permitted the priest to determine which direction the boil would take.

There is always the danger of old sins spreading and becoming malignant. Often a new convert speaks of deliverance from some evil habit and then years later that old sore may break out again. It does happen. The person who has had such an experience may have been unsaved all along, or he may have been genuinely saved but the old flesh is reappearing. A careful inspection should be made and no cursory judgment is to be pronounced.

Several years ago, a man who was an alcoholic accepted Christ as his Savior. Then he got sick and I went to visit him. I found out he wasn't really sick of anything. The place reeked of alcohol. He began to weep and said he'd slipped back. May I say to you, one might feel like taking a fellow like that and putting him across your knee and paddling him. But that wouldn't do a bit of good. We need to make an inspection and diagnose the leprosy. But we need to tell that man that his leprosy can be cured. He has a Savior. We are not to stand there and condemn him and scold him and then leave. That would make him feel bad and make me feel bad. No one would be helped. This man needed to know that he had a Savior who would forgive him. The Savior heals the leprosy that breaks out.

> **Or if there be any flesh, in the skin whereof there is a hot burning, and the quick flesh that burneth have a white bright spot, somewhat reddish, or white;**

> **Then the priest shall look upon it: and, behold, if the hair in the bright spot be turned white, and it be in sight deeper than the skin; it is a leprosy broken out of the burning: wherefore the priest shall pronounce him unclean: it is the plague of leprosy.**

> **But if the priest look on it, and, behold, there be no white hair in the bright spot, and it be no lower than the**

other skin, but be somewhat dark; then the priest shall
shut him up seven days:

And the priest shall look upon him the seventh day: and
if it be spread much abroad in the skin, then the priest
shall pronounce him unclean: it is the plague of leprosy.

And if the bright spot stay in his place, and spread not
in the skin, but it be somewhat dark; it is a rising of the
burning, and the priest shall pronounce him clean: for
it is an inflammation of the burning [Lev. 13:24-28].

This describes a leprosy that comes from a hot burning. This hot burning is not a definite identification. It would be a burning from a hot
object or it might mean the burning of an infection that has fever in it.
At any rate, there was the danger of leprosy developing in it.

This seems to confirm the Scriptures that teach us that the flesh
must be kept under close observation, for it can break out in the most
alarming manner. "I speak after the manner of men because of the
infirmity of your flesh: for as ye have yielded your members servants
to uncleanness and to iniquity unto iniquity; even so now yield your
members servants to righteousness unto holiness" (Rom. 6:19). "But I
keep under my body, and bring it into subjection: lest that by any
means, when I have preached to others, I myself should be a casta-
way" (1 Cor. 9:27).

All of these passages teach us to watch carefully for the presence of
a pimple in the flesh. The flesh cannot please God.

DIAGNOSIS OF LEPROSY LOCATED
IN THE HEAD OR THE BEARD

If a man or woman have a plague upon the head or the
beard,

Then the priest shall see the plague: and, behold, if it be
in sight deeper than the skin; and there be in it a yellow
thin hair; then the priest shall pronounce him unclean:

it is a dry scall, even a leprosy upon the head or beard [Lev. 13:29–30].

Leprosy could break out in the most unlikely spots. If it were hidden by the hair of the head or beard, it might not be discovered for some time. Special observation must be made of leprosy in these areas. The same techniques were applied here as to any other area to determine the presence of leprosy. A yellow hair indicated that the infection was beneath the epidermis and was leprosy.

You know, sin sometimes insinuates itself in the chief places in the church, into a Sunday school teachers' meeting or a board meeting or a mission meeting. It enervates and vitiates the witness of the entire body of believers when there is sin at the head. Again, one must be careful in judging these things. There must be time to make a judgment.

And if the priest look on the plague of the scall, and, behold, it be not in sight deeper than the skin, and that there is no black hair in it; then the priest shall shut up him that hath the plague of the scall seven days:

And in the seventh day the priest shall look on the plague: and, behold, if the scall spread not, and there be in it no yellow hair, and the scall be not in sight deeper than the skin;

He shall be shaven, but the scall shall he not shave; and the priest shall shut up him that hath the scall seven days more:

And in the seventh day the priest shall look on the scall: and, behold, if the scall be not spread in the skin, nor be in sight deeper than the skin; then the priest shall pronounce him clean: and he shall wash his clothes, and be clean.

But if the scall spread much in the skin after his cleansing;

> Then the priest shall look on him: and, behold, if the scall be spread in the skin, the priest shall not seek for yellow hair; he is unclean.
>
> But if the scall be in his sight at a stay, and that there is black hair grown up therein; the scall is healed, he is clean: and the priest shall pronounce him clean [Lev. 13:31–37].

So these verses go on to show that it might not be leprosy. Here again time is taken before a judgment is made and the patient is put in quarantine for seven days and then another period of seven days if that is necessary. This should teach us that accusations against the leadership in God's work should be received with a great deal of caution. Careful investigation must be made before a decision is determined.

The priest was given ample opportunity to observe the lesions. If the lesion spread later, the priest could still declare the man unclean. On the other hand, if black hair began to grow in the lesion, the priest would pronounce the man clean.

> If a man also or a woman have in the skin of their flesh bright spots, even white bright spots;
>
> Then the priest shall look: and, behold, if the bright spots in the skin of their flesh be darkish white; it is a freckled spot that groweth in the skin; he is clean [Lev. 13:38–39].

These verses point out that a freckle is not leprosy, and then the following verses show that baldness is not leprosy, although leprosy can break out in a bald spot.

> And the man whose hair is fallen off his head, he is bald; yet is he clean.
>
> And he that hath his hair fallen off from the part of his head toward his face, he is forehead bald: yet is he clean.

And if there be in the bald head, or bald forehead, a white reddish sore; it is a leprosy sprung up in his bald head, or his bald forehead.

Then the priest shall look upon it: and, behold, if the rising of the sore be white reddish in his bald head, or in his bald forehead, as the leprosy appeareth in the skin of the flesh;

He is a leprous man, he is unclean: the priest shall pronounce him utterly unclean; his plague is in his head [Lev. 13:40–44].

DISPOSAL OF LEPERS' GARMENTS

And the leper in whom the plague is, his clothes shall be rent, and his head bare, and he shall put a covering upon his upper lip, and shall cry, Unclean, unclean [Lev. 13:45].

The garments of a leper were to be torn. He was to cover his upper lip and go about crying, "Unclean, unclean." The condition of the leper is revealed in his awful state. He was capable of transmitting the disease by contact.

The sinner spreads his sin wherever he goes! His disease is contagious and he infects others. A father has a right to live his own life as he pleases, but he has no right to take a precious son to hell with him. Many fathers are doing just that. The leper had defiled everything that was around him. That is what this teaches us. Even the garments would spread the infection. Just so, everything sin touches is defiled by it.

All the days wherein the plague shall be in him he shall be defiled; he is unclean: he shall dwell alone; without the camp shall his habitation be [Lev. 13:46].

Many sinners comfort themselves by saying they will have plenty of company in hell. Notice that the leper was alone. He was separate.

The garment also that the plague of leprosy is in, whether it be a woollen garment, or a linen garment;

Whether it be in the warp, or woof; of linen, or of woollen; whether in a skin, or in any thing made of skin;

And if the plague be greenish or reddish in the garment, or in the skin, either in the warp, or in the woof, or in any thing of skin; it is a plague of leprosy, and shall be shewed unto the priest:

And the priest shall look upon the plague, and shut up it that hath the plague seven days:

And he shall look on the plague on the seventh day: if the plague be spread in the garment, either in the warp, or in the woof, or in a skin, or in any work that is made of skin; the plague is a fretting leprosy; it is unclean.

He shall therefore burn that garment, whether warp or woof, in woollen or in linen, or any thing of skin, wherein the plague is: for it is a fretting leprosy; it shall be burnt in the fire.

And if the priest shall look, and, behold, the plague be not spread in the garment, either in the warp, or in the woof or in any thing of skin;

Then the priest shall command that they wash the thing wherein the plague is, and he shall shut it up seven days more:

And the priest shall look on the plague, after that it is washed: and, behold, if the plague have not changed his colour, and the plague be not spread; it is unclean; thou shalt burn it in the fire; it is fret inward, whether it be bare within or without.

And if the priest look, and, behold, the plague be somewhat dark after the washing of it; then he shall rend it out of the garment, or out of the skin, or out of the warp, or out of the woof:

And if it appear still in the garment, either in the warp, or in the woof, or in any thing of skin; it is a spreading plague: thou shalt burn that wherein the plague is with fire.

And the garment, either warp, or woof, or whatsoever thing of skin it be, which thou shalt wash, if the plague be departed from them, then it shall be washed the second time, and shall be clean.

This is the law of the plague of leprosy in a garment of woollen or linen, either in the warp, or woof, or any thing of skins, to pronounce it clean, or to pronounce it unclean [Lev. 13:47–59].

This is an extended passage relative to the disposing of the garments. The quality of the garment made no difference. The best garments were just as infected as the cheap garments. There is a great lesson for us to learn through this. The righteousness of man is filthy rags in God's sight. Anything a sinner does or touches is contaminated by his sin.

Even the garments of those with lesser infections were to be washed. This passage shows an amazing insight into the spread of infection. We are all as an unclean thing and we, too, need washing. Only God has the remedy for the sinner.

CHAPTER 14

THEME: Ceremonial cleansing of the leper; ceremonial cleansing of a house of leprosy; ceremonial law for cleansing of leprosy and issues of the flesh

Again I must insist that we are not being given a cure for leprosy. This is the ceremonial cleansing. In the preceding chapter we saw the details of the decisions in diagnosing the leprosy. There evidently were those lepers who were cured by the treatment of that day—whatever it was, and also there were those who were healed supernaturally. We know today there is a cure for leprosy. It is not an incurable disease, and Scripture does not present it as such. It was a terrible disease and is used to teach us tremendous spiritual lessons about sin.

This chapter casts a ray of light and hope into the darkness of the leper's plight. We note that no physician's prescription is given for the treatment and cure of leprosy. Rather, it shows the ceremonial cleansing which follows the cure. This alludes to the redemption of the sinner. The ritual is entirely symbolic, yet there is a therapeutic value in the washing and cleansing.

When a man sinned in the Garden of Eden, sin separated God and man. This barrier of sin moved in a twofold direction in that it affected both God and man. It moved upward toward God and made man guilty before a holy God. It moved downward toward man, and man became polluted and contaminated with sin. Leprosy is a picture of sin in its pollution and contamination.

The remarkable feature in this chapter is the unique ceremony of cleansing and the treatment of a plague of leprosy in a house. The house is treated as a leper, obviously emphasizing the thought of contagion.

CEREMONIAL CLEANSING OF THE LEPER
WITHOUT THE CAMP

And the Lord spake unto Moses, saying,

This shall be the law of the leper in the day of his cleansing: He shall be brought unto the priest:

And the priest shall go forth out of the camp; and the
priest shall look, and, behold, if the plague of leprosy be
healed in the leper [Lev. 14:1–3].

We notice that the priest is not going out to heal the leper but is
going out to see if he has been healed. That is important. This is the
"law of the leper in the day of his cleansing." This is a ritual which
was to be followed precisely. It is a ceremonial cleansing which followed the cure of the leprosy. The man had been pronounced a leper
by the priest. Now the priest must declare him cleansed. The priest
must go out to the leper and meet him where he is. The leper would
not dare to come into society, among the people, for he was forbidden
to do that. He was shut out. Therefore, the priest must go to him. We
find this mentioned in Luke 17:12, "and as he entered into a certain
village, there met him ten men that were lepers, which stood afar off."

There is a wonderful parallel here to the person and work of our
High Priest and Great Physician. He came forth from heaven's glory to
this sin-cursed earth where man was suffering from the leprosy of sin.
Friends, we can't go up into the society of heaven when we are lepers.
We've done well to make it to the moon, but the men didn't get rid of
their sin when they went to the moon. No, it was necessary for the
Lord Jesus to come out of heaven's glory to this earth. The hymn states
it very accurately, "Out of the ivory palaces into a world of woe." That
is His story!

There is a great deal of emphasis placed on this. The second chapter of Hebrews tells about this: "But we see Jesus, who was made a
little lower than the angels for the suffering of death, crowned with
glory and honour; that he by the grace of God should taste death for
every man. For it became him, for whom are all things, and by whom

are all things, in bringing many sons unto glory, to make the captain of their salvation perfect through sufferings. . . . Forasmuch then as the children are partakers of flesh and blood, he also himself likewise took part of the same; that through death he might destroy him that had the power of death, that is, the devil. . . . For verily he took not on him the nature of angels; but he took on him the seed of Abraham. Wherefore in all things it behoved him to be made like unto his brethren, that he might be a merciful and faithful high priest in things pertaining to God, to make reconciliation for the sins of the people" (Heb. 2:9–10, 14, 16–17). He came out of heaven's glory, down to this earth. The Priest had to come to the leper! "But when the fulness of the time was come, God sent forth his Son, made of a woman, made under the law, to redeem them that were under the law, that we might receive the adoption of sons" (Gal. 4:4–5).

We need to emphasize that He still goes all the way to the sinner to heal his plague of sin. "Behold, I stand at the door, and knock: if any man hear my voice, and open the door, I will come in to him, and will sup with him, and he with me" (Rev. 3:20). God has declared that the heart of man is vile, and so it is God who must pronounce a man clean. He alone can cleanse. ". . . And the blood of Jesus Christ his Son cleanseth us from all sin" (1 John 1:7).

Now notice what the priest did when he came to the leper.

Then shall the priest command to take for him that is to be cleansed two birds alive and clean, and cedar wood, and scarlet, and hyssop:

And the priest shall command that one of the birds be killed in an earthen vessel over running water:

As for the living bird, he shall take it, and the cedar wood, and the scarlet, and the hyssop, and shall dip them and the living bird in the blood of the bird that was killed over the running water:

And he shall sprinkle upon him that is to be cleansed from the leprosy seven times, and shall pronounce him

clean, and shall let the living bird loose into the open field [Lev. 14:4–7].

Didn't I tell you this could be an unusual ceremony? I don't think there is anything, anywhere, as unusual as this. All other sacrifices were to be made at the altar of the tabernacle and, later, at the temple at the command of God. This is the exception. The leper was shut out from the tabernacle, and so it was necessary for the priest to come to him.

The brazen altar for the sacrifices speaks of the Cross of Christ. But, you see, that Cross had to be down here on this earth. He had to come down here to meet us where we are. Friends, we were shut out from God. We were strangers and afar off, without hope and without God in the world. He had to come here to meet us in our need.

There were two live, clean birds used in this sacrifice. Most likely they were doves. One was killed—to represent the death of Christ. The other was living—to represent the resurrection of Christ. These are the two facets of the gospel. Paul says, "For I delivered unto you first of all that which I also received, how that Christ died for our sins according to the scriptures; and that he was buried, and that he rose again the third day according to the scriptures" (1 Cor. 15:3–4). Two birds: death and resurrection!

Then notice that they used cedar wood. This, I think, is a symbol of the perfect humanity of Christ. The wood was incorruptible. It served a practical purpose as the handle of a brush to which the hyssop was tied with the scarlet ring. The scarlet was evidently scarlet wool.

The scarlet, I believe, is the sign of faith in the blood. It reminds us that Rahab was instructed to put out a scarlet cord as an evidence of her faith.

Hyssop is a plant that grows upon rocks in damp places. It represents the faith of the individual. "Purge me with hyssop, and I shall be clean: wash me, and I shall be whiter than snow" (Ps. 51:7). It is the appropriation and the application of the redemption in Christ. You see, one can stand at the sidelines and nod his head and say he believes that Jesus died and rose again. That is not saving faith. The question is whether or not you have appropriated it for yourself. Have you actually put your trust in Him? Also it is the application of the death of Christ and the blood of Christ to sin in the believer's life. "But if we walk in the light, as he is in the light, we have fellowship one with another, and the blood of Jesus Christ his Son cleanseth us from all sin" (1 John 1:7).

The earthen vessel speaks of the humanity of Christ. He took upon Himself our flesh, our humanity. Paul calls himself an earthen vessel in 2 Corinthians 4:7. The earthen vessel is this body which we have. The emphasis is upon the weakness and infirmity of humanity. "For we have not an high priest which cannot be touched with the feeling of our infirmities; but was in all points tempted like as we are, yet without sin" (Heb. 4:15).

Running water is living water. This water was taken from a running stream or fountain. This speaks of both the Word of God and the Spirit of God.

The ritual is both unusual and beautiful. One of the birds is slain over the earthen vessel in which there is the living water. This represents the death of Christ who offered Himself by the eternal Spirit. "How much more shall the blood of Christ, who through the eternal Spirit offered himself without spot to God, purge your conscience from dead works to serve the living God?" (Heb. 9:14).

It was essential to have the two birds to carry out the typical meaning of resurrection. The live bird was dipped in the blood of the slain bird to identify him with the bird that was slain. Then the live bird was given its freedom, permitting it to fly away. Christ was delivered for our offenses and raised for our justification to give us the liberty to stand steadfast in Christ. "Stand fast therefore in the liberty wherewith Christ hath made us free, and be not entangled again with the yoke of bondage" (Gal. 5:1). That means not to get entangled again with religion and regulations and ritual and law. Christ took our place, died our death, paid our penalty. He was raised for us. If He died for us down here, then we died in Him (2 Cor. 5:14–15) and we were raised in Him and we are in Him up yonder at the right hand of God (Eph. 1:1–6). Friends, the believer is as free as the birds of the heavens and is delivered from religion and ritual and law. The believer is now the bond-slave of the Lord Jesus Christ. He is subject to Christ's will and way. "If ye love me, keep my commandments" (John 14:15).

"He shall sprinkle upon him that is to be cleansed from the leprosy seven times." Seven is the number of completeness and finality. This settled forever the question of whether the leper was cleansed or not. There are only two kinds of people in this world, friends—there are lepers and cleansed lepers. That is, there are lost sinners and saved sinners. That is all.

Living water and blood meet in this ceremony. John was careful to note for us that when Christ died and the soldier pierced His side, blood and water came forth (John 19:34–35). He repeats the fact that Jesus Christ came by water and the blood in his epistle (1 John 5:6).

The Gnostics in John's day taught that Jesus was not God but that God came upon Him at baptism (that is the water) and departed from Him at the Cross (that is the blood). John insists that Jesus Christ was God from the very beginning when He was made flesh and that He was God on the Cross when He shed His precious blood. "And there are three that bear witness in earth, the Spirit, and the water, and the blood: and these three agree in one" (1 John 5:8). The ceremony and offering concerning the leper bore this out and illustrates this great truth.

> **And he that is to be cleansed shall wash his clothes, and shave off all his hair, and wash himself in water, that he may be clean: and after that he shall come into the camp, and shall tarry abroad out of his tent seven days.**

> **But it shall be on the seventh day, that he shall shave all his hair off his head and his beard and his eyebrows, even all his hair he shall shave off: and he shall wash his clothes, also he shall wash his flesh in water, and he shall be clean [Lev. 14:8–9].**

Now you'll have to admit that this is unusual also. The sacrificial ceremony has been completed denoting that the leper has been cleansed and accepted. Now, before he enters back into society, this further ritual shows that his old life has ended for him and a new life opens before him. The clothes represent the habits of life, his life style. The shaving off of all the hair of his body emphasizes the radical and revolutionary change that is taking place in his life.

Friends, when a believer comes to Christ, there is going to be a change! The putting away of the flesh is essential to a consistent walk before the world. The Lord Jesus said, "Ye shall know them by their fruits" (Matt. 7:16). That is still the test tube for His own.

Again, the seven days indicate a complete cycle of testing and inspection. He is to be tested before he returns to society. I think that sometimes we let new converts give a testimony too soon. Believers are to be put up and watched for a while. There must be a newness of life.

At the end of this time, he washed himself thoroughly. The child of God needs to be continually washed. "Now ye are clean through the word which I have spoken unto you" (John 15:3). "Sanctify them through thy truth: thy word is truth" (John 17:17). Friend, you can never be cleansed or sanctified, set apart for God's use, until you are saturated with the Word of God. How important that is!

May I say that the seven days for the believer, the time of completeness, is when God completes the earthly journey of His church. Then He will present her to Himself as a cleansed church (Eph. 5:25–27). In the meantime the believer is in the process of being sanctified. This is the practical aspect. There should be a daily growth, a development in faith and in practice. Holiness is to the spiritual life what health is to the physical body.

CEREMONIAL CLEANSING OF THE LEPER WITHIN THE CAMP

And on the eighth day he shall take two he lambs without blemish, and one ewe lamb of the first year without blemish, and three tenth deals of fine flour for a meat offering, mingled with oil, and one log of oil [Lev. 14:10].

The cleansed leper is now fit to enter the congregation of the Lord, but when he does, he must take his place with the other Israelites and present the offerings that every member of the congregation brought before the Lord. He brings two he lambs, one ewe lamb, fine flour, oil, and a log of oil. These are all the offerings which the average Israelite would normally make in his lifetime. It indicated the full acceptance of the cleansed leper.

And the priest that maketh him clean shall present the man that is to be made clean, and those things, before the LORD, at the door of the tabernacle of the congregation:

And the priest shall take one he lamb, and offer him for a trespass offering, and the log of oil, and wave them for a wave offering before the LORD:

And he shall slay the lamb in the place where he shall kill the sin offering and the burnt offering, in the holy place: for as the sin offering is the priest's, so is the trespass offering: it is most holy:

And the priest shall take some of the blood of the trespass offering, and the priest shall put it upon the tip of the right ear of him that is to be cleansed, and upon the thumb of his right hand, and upon the great toe of his right foot:

And the priest shall take some of the log of oil, and pour it into the palm of his own left hand:

And the priest shall dip his right finger in the oil that is in his left hand, and shall sprinkle of the oil with his finger seven times before the LORD:

And of the rest of the oil that is in his hand shall the priest put upon the tip of the right ear of him that is to be cleansed, and upon the thumb of his right hand, and

upon the great toe of his right foot, upon the blood of the
trespass offering:

And the remnant of the oil that is in the priest's hand he
shall pour upon the head of him that is to be cleansed:
and the priest shall make an atonement for him before
the LORD.

And the priest shall offer the sin offering, and make an
atonement for him that is to be cleansed from his uncleanness; and afterward he shall kill the burnt offering:

And the priest shall offer the burnt offering and the meat
offering upon the altar: and the priest shall make an
atonement for him, and he shall be clean [Lev.
14:11–20].

This extended passage in the Authorized Version is in a single sentence. The action here is one continuous ceremony which encom-
passes all the offerings and means that the cleansed leper now stands
before the door of the tabernacle just as any other Israelite.

He brings a he lamb for a trespass offering to remind him that he is
still a sinner who sins and who needs the cleansing blood of Christ
applied by the Holy Spirit to his life. The other he lamb is for a sin
offering, because the cleansed leper still has his sin nature. The ewe
lamb is for a burnt offering to set forth the person of Christ as God sees
Him. The fine flour mingled with oil speaks of the meal offering
which sets forth the loveliness of the humanity of Christ. The blood
put upon the tip of his right ear indicates that he can now hear the
voice of the Son of God saying, "Thy faith hath made thee whole." The
blood on the right thumb indicates that with clean hands he can now
serve God. The blood on his right toe indicates that the cleansed leper
can now walk in the way of God. The oil poured on his head indicates
he is now totally dedicated to God.

All these offerings speak of Christ, through whom the cleansed
leper is acceptable to God. There is nothing special about him just

because he is a cleansed leper. Too often we see Christians who feel
that somehow they are different and special. They withdraw from the
others and think they are better than the others. My friend, we each
must come just as all the rest come. Everyone must be acceptable to
God through Christ. We each need to be washed. You remember that
Peter protested to the Lord Jesus that He would never wash his feet.
Our Lord answered, ". . . If I wash thee not, thou hast no part with me"
(John 13:8). There is a great lesson in this for you and for me. Yes, the
leper was brought back and yes, he had been cleansed of his leprosy,
but he stood with the rest of the congregation before God. He still
stood as a sinner and he needed the constant cleansing before God.

Verses 21–32 explain the offering he could bring if he were poor. It
would be logical to think that a person who had been a leper would
not be able to afford an elaborate ritual. Again, the provision of God
for the poor is marvelous. No one is shut out because of poverty. Turtledoves or pigeons could be substituted in the offering.

> **And if he be poor, and cannot get so much; then he shall
> take one lamb for a trespass offering to be waved, to
> make an atonement for him, and one tenth deal of fine
> flour mingled with oil for a meat offering, and a log of
> oil;**

> **And two turtledoves, or two young pigeons, such as he
> is able to get; and the one shall be a sin offering, and the
> other a burnt offering.**

> **And he shall bring them on the eighth day for his
> cleansing unto the priest, unto the door of the tabernacle
> of the congregation, before the LORD.**

> **And the priest shall take the lamb of the trespass offer-
> ing, and the log of oil, and the priest shall wave them for
> a wave offering before the LORD:**

> **And he shall kill the lamb of the trespass offering, and
> the priest shall take some of the blood of the trespass**

offering, and put it upon the tip of the right ear of him that is to be cleansed, and upon the thumb of his right hand, and upon the great toe of his right foot:

And the priest shall pour of the oil into the palm of his own left hand:

And the priest shall sprinkle with his right finger some of the oil that is in his left hand seven times before the LORD:

And the priest shall put of the oil that is in his hand upon the tip of the right ear of him that is to be cleansed, and upon the thumb of his right hand, and upon the great toe of his right foot, upon the place of the blood of the trespass offering:

And the rest of the oil that is in the priest's hand he shall put upon the head of him that is to be cleansed, to make an atonement for him before the LORD.

And he shall offer the one of the turtledoves, or of the young pigeons, such as he can get;

Even such as he is able to get, the one for a sin offering, and the other for a burnt offering, with the meat offering: and the priest shall make an atonement for him that is to be cleansed before the LORD.

This is the law of him in whom is the plague of leprosy, whose hand is not able to get that which pertaineth to his cleansing [Lev. 14:21–32].

CEREMONIAL CLEANSING OF A HOUSE WHEREIN HAS BEEN LEPROSY

And the LORD spake unto Moses and unto Aaron, saying,

When ye be come into the land of Canaan, which I give
to you for a possession, and I put the plague of leprosy
in a house of the land of your possession;

And he that owneth the house shall come and tell the
priest, saying, It seemeth to me there is as it were a
plague in the house:

Then the priest shall command that they empty the
house, before the priest go into it to see the plague, that
all that is in the house be not made unclean: and afterward the priest shall go in to see the house [Lev.
14:33–36].

I must confess that a house would be an unusual place to find leprosy.
It is hard to know exactly what this meant. Perhaps it was some fun-
gus growth or dry rot which entered into the fabric of the house. The
priest would examine the house for greenish or reddish streaks and
would examine it again in seven days to see if the plague were spreading.

The picture is that we live in an old house down here, which is our
body. And we live in this world which is also contaminated by sin.
The old house we live in is filled with leprosy.

There are three stages in the ceremonial cleansing of the house.
First, the house was emptied of the furniture and occupants. The
priest inspected it and then shut it up for seven days before making
another inspection. If he then found a trace of leprosy, he removed the
plaster from the infected part and took away the diseased stones.

And if the plague come again, and break out in the
house, after that he hath taken away the stones, and
after he hath scraped the house, and after it is plastered;

Then the priest shall come and look, and, behold, if the
plague be spread in the house, it is a fretting leprosy in
the house: it is unclean.

And he shall break down the house, the stones of it, and
the timber thereof, and all the mortar of the house; and
he shall carry them forth out of the city into an unclean
place.

Moreover he that goeth into the house all the while that
it is shut up shall be unclean until the even.

And he that lieth in the house shall wash his clothes;
and he that eateth in the house shall wash his clothes
[Lev. 14:43–47].

If the priest found remnants of the infection in the renovated house,
then the house was to be demolished and removed.

You know, there will be a time when God will demolish this earth
that is tainted with leprosy. He is going to make it clean. There will be
a new heaven and a new earth and they will be free from sin.

And if the priest shall come in, and look upon it, and,
behold, the plague hath not spread in the house, after
the house was plastered; then the priest shall pronounce
the house clean, because the plague is healed [Lev.
14:48].

The same ritual of the two birds is followed here as in the case of the
ceremonial cleansing of the leper.

And he shall take to cleanse the house two birds, and
cedar wood, and scarlet, and hyssop:

And he shall kill the one of the birds in an earthen vessel over running water:

And he shall take the cedar wood, and the hyssop, and
the scarlet, and the living bird, and dip them in the
blood of the slain bird, and in the running water, and
sprinkle the house seven times:

And he shall cleanse the house with the blood of the
bird, and with the running water, and with the living
bird, and with the cedar wood, and with the hyssop,
and with the scarlet:

But he shall let go the living bird out of the city into the
open fields, and make an atonement for the house: and it
shall be clean [Lev. 14:49–53].

CEREMONIAL LAW FOR CLEANSING OF LEPROSY AND ISSUES OF THE FLESH

This is the law for all manner of plague of leprosy, and
scall,

And for the leprosy of a garment, and of a house,

And for a rising, and for a scab, and for a bright spot:

To teach when it is unclean, and when it is clean: this is
the law of leprosy [Lev. 14:54–57].

This seems to be an emphatic enforcement of the law concerning the
cleansing of the leprosy. Notice that the primary purpose of the ritual
was to teach. "To teach when it is unclean, and when it is clean."

This is a great spiritual lesson and it is meant to teach us. You and I
have spiritual leprosy. If either you or I went to heaven without Jesus
Christ, without trusting Him, we would cry out, "Unclean, unclean,"
and we would be cast out. In Christ, we are accepted in the Beloved!
My friend, where are you today? Are you a leper who has come to
Jesus Christ for cleansing or are you still unclean?

BIBLIOGRAPHY
(Recommended for Further Study)

Gaebelein, Arno C. *Annotated Bible*, Vol. 1. Neptune, New Jersey: Loizeaux Brothers, 1917.

Goldberg, Louis. *Leviticus*. Grand Rapids, Michigan: Zondervan Publishing House, 1980.

Grant, F. W. *Numerical Bible*. Neptune, New Jersey: Loizeaux Brothers, 1891.

Gray, James M. *Synthetic Bible Studies*. Westwood, New Jersey: Fleming H. Revell Co., 1906.

Heslop, W. G. *Lessons from Leviticus*. Grand Rapids, Michigan: Kregel Publications, 1945.

Ironside, H. A. *Lectures on the Levitical Offerings*. Neptune, New Jersey: Loizeaux Brothers, 1929.

Jamieson, Robert; Faucett H. R.; and Brown, D. *Commentary on the Bible*. 3 vols. Grand Rapids, Michigan: Wm. B. Eerdmans Publishing Co., 1945.

Jensen, Irving L. *Leviticus*. Chicago, Illinois: Moody Press, 1967.

Jukes, Andrew. *The Law of the Offerings*. Grand Rapids, Michigan: Kregel Publications, 1870.

Kellogg, S. H. *The Book of Leviticus*. New York: George H. Doran Co., 1908.

Kelly, William. *Lectures Introductory to the Pentateuch*. Oak Park, Illinois: Bible Truth Publishers, 1870.

Mackintosh, C. H. (C.H.M.). *Notes on the Pentateuch*. Neptune, New Jersey: Loizeaux Brothers, 1880.

McGee, J. Vernon. *Learning Through Leviticus.* 2 vols. Pasadena, California: Thru the Bible Books, 1964.

Noordtzij, A. *Leviticus.* Grand Rapids, Michigan: Zondervan Publishing House, 1982.

Slemming, C. W. *These Are the Garments.* London, England: Marshall Morgan & Scott, n.d.

Slemming, C. W. *Thus Shalt Thou Serve.* Fort Washington, Pennsylvania: Christian Literature Crusade, 1955.

Shultz, Samuel J. *Leviticus.* Chicago, Illinois: Moody Press, 1983.

Thomas, W. H. Griffith. *Through the Pentateuch Chapter by Chapter.* Grand Rapids, Michigan: Wm. B. Eerdmans Publishing Co., 1957.

Unger, Merrill F. *Unger's Bible Handbook.* Chicago, Illinois: Moody Press, 1966.

Unger, Merrill F. *Unger's Commentary on the Old Testament,* Vol. I. Chicago, Illinois: Moody Press, 1981.